The Plai[ntiff and] Defense Attorney's Guide to Understanding Economic Damages

Michael L. Brookshire
Frank Slesnick
John O. Ward

Contributors

George A. Barrett
Elizabeth A.W. Gunderson
John D. Hancock
R. Edison Hill
Kurt V. Krueger
Gerald Martin
Ann T. Neulicht

Jeffrey B. Opp
William A. Posey
James D. Rodgers
E. Wayne Taff
Robert H. Taylor
Robert J. Thornton
Howard H. Vogel

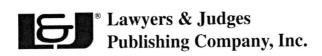
Lawyers & Judges
Publishing Company, Inc.

Lawyers & Judges
Publishing Company, Inc.

P.O. Box 30040 • Tucson, AZ 85751-0040
(800) 209-7109 • FAX (800) 330-8795
e-mail: sales@lawyersandjudges.com
www.lawyersandjudges.com

Library of Congress Cataloging-in-Publication Data

Brookshire, Michael L.
 The plaintiff and defense attorney's guide to understanding economic damages / Michael L. Brookshire, Frank Slesnick, and John O. Ward ; contributors, George A. Barrett ... [et al.].
   p. cm.
 ISBN-13: 978-1-933264-10-3 (pbk. : alk. paper)
 ISBN-10: 1-933264-10-1 (pbk. : alk. paper)
 1. Damages--United States--Trial practice. 2. Lost earnings damages--United States--Trial practice. 3. Trial practice--United States. 4. Forensic economics--United States. I. Slesnick, Frank. II. Ward, John O. III. Barrett, George A. IV. Title.
 KF8925.D36B765 2007
 347.73'77--dc22

2007014674

ISBN 978-1-933264-10-3
ISBN 1-933264-10-1
Printed in the United States of America
10 9 8 7 6 5 4 3

Dedication

*This book is dedicated to our wives Pam, Sue, and Lynn
and to our colleagues and friends in the
National Association of Forensic Economics.*

John Ward
Frank Slesnick
Mike Brookshire

Table of Contents

Introduction

Whether you are representing the plaintiff or defendant in personal injury or wrongful death litigation, remember that the use of damages experts' opinions can be a house of cards or foundation of strength. The chapters in this book represent the individual opinions of nationally known attorneys, economists, vocational rehabilitation experts, and life care planners. The three co-editors of this book have over ninety years of combined experience as forensic economic experts. Each has served as a university professor and past president of the National Association of Forensic Economics. The contributing authors to this book have been selected because of their leadership roles in their fields of law, vocational evaluation, economics, and life care planning and their practical experience in personal injury and death litigation. Our collective goal, in writing this book, has been to create a practical guide to the use of damages experts in personal injury and death litigation—a guide that is equally useful to defense and plaintiff lawyers.

Over the past decade a number of books, written by either economists or attorneys, have approached the topic of using damages experts effectively in PI/death litigation. Such books have been primarily directed to other economists, with an emphasis on methodological issues of interest to forensic economists. Books written by attorneys have emphasized legal damages issues of interest to attorneys. This book is unique in that it combines these interests and focus them at the practical issues faced by attorneys in using, and trying to understand, damages experts.

While the book has been written for attorneys, it is also a resource for damages experts who are interested in improving their skills and understanding the legal perspective of their work. Good forensic economists, vocational experts, and life care planners have to understand their roles and limitations in the litigation process and this book, hopefully, provides such guidance from the perspectives of trial attorneys as well as damages experts. Experts should never be advocates for one side or the other, but they should be advocates for the methodologies they use, and those methodologies must meet the standards of reasonable probability to be of use.

Damages experts must maintain an independence of opinion from the interests of the attorney retaining them. Good damages experts should be as willing to tell the retaining attorney the deficiencies of the case as well as the strengths. Good attorneys should know the limitations of expert testimony and what makes a good damages expert. In the chapters that follow, nationally recognized attorneys and damages experts will present their perspectives on these issues. In addition, each chapter will be supplemented with an accompanying CD section containing some or all of the following components:

- links to internet sources of information to supplement chapters;
- definitions of technical terminology used in chapters;
- sample direct and cross-examination questions and strategies;
- case studies and sample reports supporting subjects covered in chapters; and
- references for each chapter and recommended readings in the field.

The CD will contain links that, when selected, will take the reader to the internet site containing the material emphasized. The CD will also link to internet damages calculators that will allow readers to calculate simple lost earnings and services in their own cases based on a variety of characteristics of the plaintiff.

By necessity, there are topics that cannot be examined in an introductory text and the CD will contain an index to such subjects and direct internet links to allow the reader to download relevant articles and cases of interest.

Finally, the views expressed by each contributing author are not necessarily shared by other contributing authors or the editors. Our goal in writing this book was to bring together experts and attorneys with extensive professional and leadership experience in their fields and a review of biographical statements at the end of the book attests to the achievement of that goal. Our second goal was to provide a balanced treatment of topics, both from the perspectives of plaintiffs and defendants, and we believe that goal has been achieved. Finally, our goal was to produce a highly readable and practical text on using damages experts in litigation, and judgment of that achievement rests with the readers.

Dr. Michael Brookshire, Dr. Frank Slesnick, and Dr. John Ward, co-editors

Chapter 1

Understanding Experts on Damage Valuation

John O. Ward, Ph.D.

In personal injury and death litigation, attorneys for the plaintiff and defendant will at some point have to decide whether their case will require the use of damages experts based upon the likely outcome of retaining such experts. Appealing directly to the jury for economic damages without the use of experts is certainly warranted in cases where likely economic damages and/or limits of coverage are small and liability is in serious doubt. Such cases are still probably a majority of personal injury and death cases filed with the courts. However, when damages are multifaceted and large, and coverage is substantial, the use of damages experts becomes critical to the attorney's case strategy. It is easy just to say that you will know when you need damages experts when the occasion arises. But most attorneys are not conversant in the language of damages experts and most attorneys really don't understand the process of building a damages case using such experts. They don't know how to select quality damages experts or to judge the quality, strengths, and weaknesses of a damages analysis. Your damages experts will not only provide a theory of damages, they will also assist in the litigation process by lending their names and credibility in settlement discussions. In addition, they can be valuable resources in reviewing an opposition expert's report, developing lines of questions for depositions and trial, participating in the design of settlement offers, and preparing trial exhibits.

1

The objectives of this book are to provide attorneys with some basic tools for:

1. understanding the damages experts' perspectives of their role in calculating damages;
2. understanding the basic terminology used by damages experts;
3. understanding the difference between a quality damages case and an inadequate case; and
4. understanding how to select damages experts and communicate with the experts.

The authors of the chapters in this book represent highly experienced damages experts from the fields of economics, vocational rehabilitation, and life care planning and highly successful attorneys who represent plaintiffs and defendants in personal injury and death litigation. While the attorneys are expected to be advocates for their clients and partial to their claims, the damages expert is expected to be objective and impartial. Good damages experts make that clear to the attorneys retaining them and good attorneys recognize the importance of maintaining the independence of their experts' opinions.

1.1 It Ends With Dollars

The damages case rests on establishing the dollar value to be placed on: (1) economic damages representing the harm to the plaintiff in the forms of replacing losses of earnings and fringe benefits, ability to perform services, past and future medical costs in an injury case and support to survivors or an estate in death cases; (2) non-economic damages such as pain and suffering and/or mental anguish; and (3) punitive damages if allowed.

Damages experts can be categorized as (a) those who assist in establishing the facts of damages, such as physicians and psychologists; (b) those who specify the parameters of damages, such as vocational evaluators and life care planners, and (c) economists who mathematically compute lifetime dollar amounts of economic loss. Here we are focused on those who place values on damages. You can think of the damages valuation process as a pyramid of foundation with the calculations of the economic expert on the values of damages at the apex of the pyramid. The ultimate values of damages can be no more reasonable than the foundation supporting those damages. This concept does not elevate the role of the economist or diminish the roles of other damages experts; it simply puts those roles in perspective. To best understand the damages valuation process it is easiest to start at the apex—the damages report and/or testimony of the economic expert. The damages report of the economic expert has the following structure.

1. Economic Expert Report/Testimony
2. Facts and Assumptions
3. Elements of Damages Considered
4. Sources of Foundation
5. Methodology Used
6. Damages Presentation

In fact, the damages put forward by the economist are only as valid as the analysis of damages put forward as foundation by the life care planner or the vocational expert. The garbage in, garbage out defense to an expert economist's testimony rests on this premise.

1.2 Facts and Assumptions

The report/testimony of the economic expert will necessarily rest on facts and assumptions about the plaintiff provided by others. The facts and assumptions provided to the economic expert should be clearly identified in the expert's report and/or testimony as part of the disclosure process. Material facts, such as the plaintiff's birth date, date of alleged injury, marital status, education, and employment history, can be objectively verified as to accuracy. Assumptions such as the cause of the injury or death, the impact of the injury on employability and the probable worklife expectancy of the plaintiff are subjective and may reasonably differ among economic experts. Such assumptions, when provided by a vocational expert or life care planner, are only as valid as the accuracy, diligence, and expertise of the expert providing the opinion. It is important for the attorney employing the expert to remember that each damages expert has a unique role in establishing foundation for the ultimate damages numbers and that those roles are vertically integrated like links in a chain. Economists should generally not try to offer expert opinions on vocational or life care matters, and vocational experts or life care planners similarly should generally not attempt to express economic opinions. There are some exceptions to these rules. Some experts, by training, can function in multiple roles as vocational, economic, or life care planning experts. Such people are very few in number. Some "damages experts" advertise their abilities to provide vocational, life care and economic testimony with few credentials in any of these fields. The roles of damages experts for the defense where plaintiffs have hired such suspect experts should be to attack the expertise of such experts as well as the assumptions and analysis of their work.

1.3 Elements of Damages Considered

The elements of damages considered by the economic expert may include some or all of the following items:

- loss or impairment of future earnings capacity or earnings;
- loss or reduction of past and/or future fringe benefits;
- loss or impairment of ability to perform household services in the past or future;
- past medical costs related to the alleged injury;
- future medical costs and life care needs resulting from the alleged harm;
- lost value of care, advice, and counsel provided to survivors;
- lost enjoyment of life of person harmed to self or survivors; and
- losses of active income from business or investment activities unique to the person harmed.

The above damages categories represent common economic damages in most state and federal courts, although the loss of enjoyment of life and the lost values of care, advice, and counsel are considered in some jurisdictions. The selection of categories of damages to measure is determined by the facts and assumptions of the case and the legal definition of economic damages in the jurisdiction. A strategy of the retaining attorney is to select damages categories to be measured and presented by experts. For example, even if lost household services are allowed as economic damages in the jurisdiction and the expert is capable and willing to measure such damages, a decision by the retaining attorney that such a presentation would compromise his case might dictate their exclusion. For each damages area selected for expert testimony, the attorney must make sure that his economic expert expresses an independent opinion on damages resting on the constraints of the law and the facts of the case.

1.4 Sources of Foundation

The economic expert, as previously stated, is at the apex of the damages triangle and is usually the final voice for the plaintiff or defendant on damages. Whether the jury agrees with that voice, or is even allowed to hear that voice, is a function of the existence of a foundation for the expert's opinion. The foundation for a damages calculation may come from:

1. direct interview(s) by the expert with the injured person, survivors of a deceased plaintiff, employers (pre- and post-injury) or other "fact" witnesses;

2. responses to questionnaires or interrogatories submitted by the expert, plaintiff or defendant;
3. depositions of fact witnesses and case pleadings;
4. tax returns, W-2s, fringe benefit statements, pay-stubs, employment records and Social Security records on earnings;
5. union seniority lists, employment contracts, and pay schedules;
6. reports by CPAs or tax preparers on business income and expenses;
7. medical treatment documents detailing the nature of the injury;
8. past medical payments records;
9. in injury cases, any records of disability insurance appraisal (Employer or Social Security);
10. specific records of job search and results and statements by physicians on employment disability;
11. in injury cases, evaluations, reports, and depositions by vocational/rehabilitation experts;
12. in injury cases, life care plans by life care planners;
13. in injury cases, evaluations, reports, and depositions by psychological experts on loss of enjoyment of life;
14. statistical sources of information on life expectancies, probabilities of labor force participation, unemployment probabilities, wage trends, hours worked trends, household services performed, time-use data on care, advice, and counsel, fringe benefit rates by industry, interest rates, inflation rates and other socio-economic factors; and
15. statements by retaining attorneys of specific "hypotheticals" to be incorporated in the report of elements of damages to be included.

It is incumbent on the economic expert to do "due diligence" in gathering such information, requesting such information and disclosing such information in reports and testimony. The same is true of the vocational expert and the life care planner in their analysis. However, it is not the responsibility of the economic expert to gather "all" of the foundation listed above. The economic expert should gather "enough" foundation to support conclusions with reasonable probability. Information from different sources can be, and often is, redundant. W-2s alone can provide a reasonable basis for projecting future earnings in a specific case and a questionnaire alone can provide a reasonable basis for projecting lost household services in specific cases. In a world of unlimited budgets and time for gathering foundation, an expert might gather all of the foundation elements listed above. In a world of limited budgets and time, the economic expert should gather as much foundation as "necessary" to support her conclusions on damages. There are no bright lines on where that sufficiency exists.

Items 1 through 10 are of varying importance in establishing foundation. It is not necessary to conduct personal interviews with fact witnesses, and most economic experts do not conduct such interviews. Rather, they rely on written response to questionnaires, depositions, and tax documents in outlining the facts of a case. However, an interview often can enhance the foundation considered, and will enhance the image of "due diligence" of the expert. At trial, under cross-examination, a question that "you never even took the time to talk to the plaintiff" may just be posturing, but it can be effective posturing.

Items 11 through 13 apply to personal injury cases where an earnings record is lacking, mitigation of earnings loss is an issue, future medical care is needed or a claim is made for loss of enjoyment of life. Relatively few economists deal with loss of enjoyment of life because of legal restraints, perceived methodological deficiencies in measuring such damages or beliefs that they are non-economic damages. The economic expert is not a vocational specialist (in most cases) and is not a life care planner (in most cases). Those economists who have such talents are rare. Economists should not be asked to, nor attempt to, translate medical records into occupational disabilities. In most cases, where the injured person has residual earnings capacity or that issue is in doubt, the attorney should retain a vocational expert who can test the plaintiff, review employment and medical records, and offer opinion on pre-injury earnings capacity and post-injury earnings capacity. Similarly, if future medical costs and care are an issue, a life care planner should be retained to establish future medical needs, costs and duration for the economic expert. The economist can then reduce that plan to present value for the jury. The economist can project limited future medical costs based on hypotheticals provided by the attorney, but such projections should generally be avoided absent support from a medical expert.

Item 14 is fundamental to all economic projections and is an area that will be challenged by opposing economic experts. While Bureau of Labor Statistics (BLS) data, Census data, and U.S. Public Health data are relied upon as authoritative by economists, the use of that data is subject to manipulation by choice and use. Some economic experts use minimal statistical data and conclusions to support their positions, and their analysis, as such, is subject to challenge through lack of reasonable probability standards and *Daubert* challenges. Again, there are no bright lines on the use of statistical data in making projections. The expert has to anticipate challenges, be comfortable with the standard of reasonable probability and be able to explain why the data she selected was consistent with that standard.

Item 15 is troublesome for economic experts when, for example, the hypothetical is not supportable within the facts of the case or subject to reasonable probability of occurrence. Nevertheless, it is appropriate for a retaining attorney to ask the expert to make a specific calculation and for the expert to make such a calculation as long as that attorney-supplied assumption or hypothetical fact is disclosed in the expert's report and testimony. Even though the particular economic expert uses Social Security retirement age in projecting lost earnings, the attorney can request a projection to age seventy, for example, based on the intent of his client. The economist might make two projections, one to Social Security retirement age and the second to age seventy. The second projection should be identified as a hypothetical requested by the attorney. The opposing attorney is always free to request any other age of retirement calculation, through her own expert or through cross-examination at trial.

1.5 Methodology Used

The story goes that if you locked five economists in a room and asked them to come to a conclusion on a topic, you would wind up with five separate conclusions. You could substitute vocational or life care experts for economists in the story. There are a number of variables that go into projecting any of the elements of economic loss discussed above, and a number of ways of incorporating such variables in a loss calculation. As an example, a projection of lost earnings in an injury case involves the selection of an earnings base from which to begin; the selection of which fringe benefits, if any, to add to loss; the length of time to project loss; adjustments to loss for voluntary and involuntary risks of labor force participation and employment; changes in earnings likely to occur because of wage growth due to advancement, productivity increases and demand shifts for labor and inflation; adjustments, if any, to be made for collateral sources of income or taxes; and the discounting of loss for interest that could be earned on the investment of an award over the period of loss. The treatment of each of these steps in the calculation could vary based on whether earnings capacity or probable earnings were the standards of loss, whether real or nominal growth and discounting were utilized, whether age earnings cycle trends are considered, whether projections are based on historical trends or current economic conditions, and the legal rules for the treatment of damages in the specific jurisdiction. So, it is not surprising that two economists would have different conclusions on economic damages in a specific case. Nevertheless, it is not unusual for projections in a specific case by two competent economists with the same base assumptions to fall within a fairly narrow range. This is true because the past twenty years has seen substantial research into the forensic economic methodology, the publication of substantial literature on such methodologies in the *Journal of Forensic Economics, the Journal of Legal Economics,* and other journals, and the publication of a number of books in the field. Each year, up to eight regional, national, and international conferences of forensic economists are held, with numerous presentations on issues of methodology. There is an emerging and evolving consensus on the components of a valid earnings loss forecast, subject to the law in a specific jurisdiction and the facts of a case. A uniformity of methodology is neither possible nor desirable. Economists will continue to disagree on choices of worklife, earnings growth rates, discount rates, and other methodological components. However, the ranges of methodological choices are well known and increasingly predictable.

The Statement of Ethical Principles and Principles of Professional Practice of the National Association of Forensic Economics (NAFE) contains four standards relative to methodologies used in damages calculations that are:

1. Diligence

Practitioners of forensic economics should employ generally accepted and/or theoretically sound economic methodologies based on reliable economic data. Practitioners of forensic economics should attempt to provide accurate, fair, and reasonable expert opinions, recognizing that it is not the responsibility of the practitioner to verify the accuracy or completeness of the case-specific information that has been provided.

2. Disclosure

Practitioners of forensic economics should stand ready to provide sufficient detail to allow replication of all numerical calculations, with reasonable effort, by other competent forensic economics experts, and be prepared to provide sufficient disclosure of sources of information and assumptions underpinning their opinions to make them understandable to others.

3. Consistency

While it is recognized that practitioners of forensic economics may be given a different assignment when engaged on behalf of the plaintiff than when engaged on behalf of the defense, for any given assignment the basic assumptions, sources, and methods should not change, regardless of the party who engages the expert to perform the assignment. There should be no change in methodology for purposes of favoring any party's claim. This requirement of consistency is not meant to preclude methodological changes as new knowledge evolves, nor is it meant to preclude performing requested calculations based upon a hypothetical—as long as its hypothetical nature is clearly disclosed in the expert's report and testimony.

4. Knowledge
Practitioners of forensic economics should strive to maintain a current knowledge base of their discipline.

In joining NAFE, a forensic economist must accept the above ethical standards. In reality, that does not mean that all NAFE members meet the standards of ethical practice because their work is not screened by NAFE for conformance to published ethical standards. Moreover, a significant number of practicing forensic economists are not members of NAFE. There are forensic economists who act as advocates rather than experts in their practices, who knowingly alter their methodologies to fit the needs of their clients, who rely upon dubious statistical bases, and who represent themselves as damages "illustrators." The same can be said for vocational and life care experts. In the age of *Daubert* it is wise to avoid retaining such experts.

1.6 Damages Presentation

The objective of the forensic economist is to evaluate damages suffered by a plaintiff, either for the attorney representing the plaintiff or the attorney representing the defendant. Typically, the economic expert for the plaintiff will prepare a report detailing those projections. The report should provide sufficient detail to allow a replication of the calculations by another economist. It should disclose all facts and assumptions considered, hypotheticals provided, and sources of information utilized in making the calculations. Such disclosures are necessary under the Federal Rules of Evidence and are increasingly being required in state courts. An economic expert retained by the attorney for the defendant will often be asked to offer only a critical appraisal of the methodology and values of damages offered by the economic expert for the plaintiff. The primary roles of the economist for the defendant are to provide the defense attorney with areas of attack on the validity of the expert's analysis, to write discovery and cross-examination questions, and, increasingly, to assist in preparing motions in limine to bar all or part of the other expert's testimony or to assist in preparing for a *Daubert* hearing to strike the expert's testimony altogether. To provide actual damages values for the defendant could be viewed as an endorsement of liability and a bottom line for a damages award. Where liability is probable, the economic expert for the defense is more likely to be asked to provide such damages calculations.

The same roles exist for vocational or life care experts for the plaintiff or defendant. The detail of those roles is provided in Chapters 6 and 7.

1.7 Credentials of Damages Experts

Selecting a damages expert can be a daunting process. Economic experts may not really be economists. Certified Public Accountants, business finance experts, and some vocational evaluators also offer their services as experts in the valuation of damages in personal injury and death litigation. While most economic experts have Ph.D.s in economics, many have Ph.D.s in other disciplines such as finance, or other degrees such as M.B.A.s or licenses such as CPAs. There is no certification process for economic experts, although CPAs have a certification process and the finance area is littered with certifications. Some economic experts have such dubious certifications as a "Chartered Vocational Economist."

Vocational evaluation experts have an equally confusing credentialing system. Most vocational evaluation experts come from vocation/rehabilitation backgrounds. Most vocational evaluation experts have a master's degree in counseling from schools of education and gain their experience from worker's compensation and Social Security disability compensation work. Some vocational experts have Ph.D.s in Vocational Rehabilitation and Counseling. Vocational evaluators do have a number of certification processes offered by several professional associations. One can be a Certified Vocational Evaluator (CVA), a Certified Rehabilitation Counselor (CRC), or a Certified Vocational Expert (CVE) through such organizations as the American Board of Vocational Experts, the International Association of Rehabilitation Professionals, or the Association of Vocational and Rehabilitation Counselors. What the economic expert needs from the vocational evaluator is (a) a clear statement of the plaintiff's earnings potential but for the alleged injury in cases where the individual has not yet established an earnings history and (b) a clear statement of the plaintiff's earnings potential post-injury. The report of the vocational evaluator usually will contain an employment history, medical history, and family history of the appraised, along with the results of vocational and intelligence testing and conclusions about post-injury earnings potential. Some vocational evaluators might then go on to project the lost earnings capacity of the plaintiff, although this is rare. Few vocational evaluators have the training or credentials to make such a calculation.

Life care planners provide the foundation for a calculation of funds needed to care for the injured plaintiff and to restore the plaintiff to as great a degree of independence as reasonably possible. Life care planners either come from medical backgrounds or vocational backgrounds. Registered nurses enter into the field of life care planning from their experience in nursing and specialized training in life care planning. Colleges offer certificates and graduate degrees in the field of life care planning for both registered nurses and vocational/rehabilitation professionals. Such certificates include the Certified Nurse Life Care Planner (CNLCP) and the Certified Life Care Planner (CLCP). The life care plan should include only those care items made necessary by the alleged injuries sustained by the plaintiff, and should not include other care items due to other medical conditions. It is the responsibility of the life care planner to review all medical records of the plaintiff, typically to interview the plaintiff, and to obtain the approval of treating and retained medical experts for items contained in the life care plan. The life care plan should include the items needed, the length of time needed, the frequency of use, and base cost of the item. The economic expert will project the present value of the costs of such items to a statistical life expectancy or a life expectancy specific to the plaintiff, as provided by medical testimony.

1.8 Where Do You Find Quality Experts?

First, consider what you mean by a quality expert. There are highly successful and well-known economic, vocational, and life care experts who promise to provide the results desired by their hiring attorney—avoid them. Such experts are also well known to qualified experts in their fields; they may have track records of ethics violation complaints; they usually have past testimony barred by a judge; and they are walking targets for *Daubert* hearings. Some experts advertise their services in ATLA or various bar associations' publications. Some experts list their services as sub-contractors through services such as TASA. While such experts may be qualified, it is generally better to select an expert based on recommendations of other attorneys. You find excellent experts by asking excellent attorneys who they use and why they use them. Frequently, experts make presentations to bar association and law school CLE programs. Quality damages experts are good teachers. They have strong professional credentials with records of publication in their fields of expertise. They are consistent in their work as experts—they work for both plaintiffs and defendants and they are strong advocates for their analysis, not the positions of the attorneys who retain them. They ask a lot of questions and they want sufficient foundation for their opinions. They respectfully consider your views on damages and they will incorporate hypotheticals you provide in their analysis if requested. But, your hypotheticals will be identified as such and their analysis will fully be their work. Their conclusions will be replicable by other experts and it will disclose all facts considered, assumptions used, and methodologies employed. Your goal is to have an expert whose opinions are *Daubert*-proof.

Economic experts usually start as university faculty who develop an interest in forensic economics and serve as experts in a limited number of cases. Some of these small practices become large practices with the passage of time. Some economic experts start as economic experts, working for large consulting or accounting firms. Most economic experts have a Ph.D. in economics or finance. Some only have an M.A. or M.B.A. degree, but have substantial experience in the field. A number of economic experts are not economists at all—they are CPAs. While CPAs traditionally have focused on commercial litigation, a number have established strong credentials as experts in personal injury or death litigation. As stated earlier, there is no credentialing process for economic experts, unlike vocational and life care experts. In following chapters, prominent trial attorneys will discuss their criteria for finding excellent damages experts. It can be a minefield.

1.9 The *Daubert* Age

Just like the economic expert, the opinions of vocational evaluators and life care planners rest on foundations of fact, opinion, statistics, assumptions, and hypotheticals. Each of these experts will use a methodology to arrive at her conclusions. All sources of information considered should be disclosed in her reports and testimony and methodologies used will be judged by the standards of the profession and the consistency of the individual expert in using that methodology.

The final calculation of economic damages in a case rests on the foundation considered by the economic expert and the methodology utilized by the expert. The courts are becoming more demanding of the quality of that foundation and the scientific basis for the methodology used. In federal courts, questions asked about the statistical reliability of estimates and margins of error are increasingly common. To meet these challenges, it is incumbent on the attorney to understand the concepts of "reasonable probability" and known margins of error—especially if confronted by a *Daubert* hearing to bar your expert's testimony.

Rule 702 of the Federal Rules of Evidence states that "if scientific, technical, or other specialized knowledge will assist the trier of fact to understand the evidence or to determine a fact in issue, a witness qualified as an expert by knowledge, skill, experience, training, or education, may testify thereto in the form of an opinion or otherwise, if (1) the testimony is based upon sufficient facts or data, (2) the testimony is the product of reliable principles and methods, and (3) the witness has applied the principles and methods reliably to the facts of the case."

For many years, the admissibility of expert scientific evidence was governed by the *Frye* test, a common law rule of thumb named after a 1923 decision by the District of Columbia Court of Appeals (*Frye v. United States* 54 App D.C. 46, 293 F1013 (1923)). Under the *Frye* test, expert scientific evidence was admissible only if the principles on which it was based had gained "general acceptance" in the scientific community. The *Frye* test still remains in most state courts, but it has been replaced in Federal court and a growing number of state courts.

In 1992 in *Daubert* (*Daubert v. Merrill Dow Pharmaceuticals* (92-102) 509 U.S. 579 (1993)), the Supreme Court was asked to decide whether the *Frye* test had been replaced by the adoption, in 1973, of the *Federal Rules of Evidence,* particularly Rule 702. This did not even mention "general acceptance," but simply provided "If scientific, technical, or other specialized knowledge will assist the trier of fact to understand the evidence or to determine a fact in issue, a witness qualified as an expert by knowledge, skill, experience, training, or education, may testify thereto in the form of an opinion or otherwise."

The majority opinion in *Daubert* held that Rule 702 did indeed supplant *Frye.* This did not mean, however, that all expert testimony purporting to be scientific was now to be admissible. Rule 702 did require that the testimony actually be founded on "scientific knowledge." This implied that the testimony must be grounded in the *methods and procedures* of science—"the scientific method." Evidence thus grounded, said the Court, would possess the requisite *scientific* validity to establish an acceptable level of reliability. An excellent discussion of the movement from *Frye* to *Daubert*, a full statement of the *Daubert* decision and the application of *Daubert* to expert testimony is contained in the web page of the Legal Information Institute http://www.daubertontheweb.com/frye_opinion.htm of The Cornell Law School. In *Daubert*, the Court explicitly refused to adopt any "definitive checklist or test" for determining the reliability of expert scientific testimony, and emphasized the need for flexibility. The Court did list several factors the courts might consider in judging the admissibility of expert testimony. Those factors include:

- whether the theories and techniques employed by the scientific expert have been tested;
- whether the expert's theories and techniques have been peer reviewed or published;
- whether such theories and techniques have a known rate of error;
- whether there are standards governing the application of such techniques; and
- whether the expert's theories and techniques have widespread acceptance among peers.

The absence of one of the above factors is not sufficient to bar the testimony of an expert and the court emphasized that the admissibility inquiry should focus on the expert's "principles and methodology," and "not on the conclusions that they generate." Even with the admissibility of such testimony the traditional tools of cross-examination and rules of evidence could be used to challenge the expert's opinions, but the new rules would allow new and novel theories to be placed before juries without the *Frye* standard of "common acceptance." In *Daubert*, the courts became the gatekeepers to the admissibility of expert scientific testimony by establishing requirements for the reliability of such testimony.

1.10 Is Economic Testimony Scientific?

Expert economic testimony on damages, like vocational or life care testimony, is technical and specialized, but not scientific in the way that much medical and engineering testimony is scientific. Known rates of error are not available for earnings loss projections or valuation of life care plans. However, in *Kumho Tire Co. v. Carmichael*, 526 U.S. 137 (1999), the Supreme Court extended the "gate-keeping" role of the courts outlined in *Daubert* to all expert testimony.

So, at least in federal courts and some state courts, the "*Daubert*" hearing has become a common tool to challenge the reliability of opinions of damages experts. It is very important that both the retaining attorney and the damages experts retained be aware of the *Daubert* criteria for admissibility of expert testimony and be prepared to produce an analysis that meets those criteria.

1.11 Conclusions

A quick review of the web pages of the National Association of Forensic Economics (NAFE), the International Association of Rehabilitation Professionals (IARP), and the various certifying bodies for life care planners and vocational experts would reveal that damages experts are very much aware of the issues that *Daubert* and tort reform present to the effective use of damages experts in the courts. Both NAFE and the IARP have embarked on efforts to clearly define the ethical and professional practice standards of their fields of study. The proliferation of "damages experts" over the past two decades, the promotion of dubious damages models by some, the growing need for demonstration of foundation for expert testimony, and the pure costs of hiring such experts has created a "minefield" for plaintiff and defense attorneys in need of such experts. The discussion above has centered on the expert's view of selecting and using damages experts, primarily economists. In the chapters that follow, these and other issues will be examined by both plaintiff and defense attorneys and other damages experts with the goals of providing the reader with an understanding of how to effectively navigate the use of damages experts in personal injury/death litigation.

Chapter 2

The Trial Attorney's View on Choosing and Using Economists and Related Experts on Damages

William A. Posey, Esq.

2.1 Why Retain an Economist?
A. Plaintiff's considerations

Attorneys representing injured parties must seek to maximize the recovery for their clients, while at the same time being cognizant of the costs required to establish and explain their damages. One of the early considerations for plaintiff's counsel is whether the case requires an economist for the appropriate presentation of the damages, and whether such an expense is justified, given the nature and extent of the potential damages. There are no golden rules on this issue. However, it is clear that when the injured party has suffered losses or damages that will continue into the future, such as lost wages, the limitation on the ability to earn income, and necessary future medical care, rehabilitation, or assistance, plaintiff's counsel must be prepared to explain how the cost or value of those losses increase in the future due to inflation, and also to reduce those calculations of future damages to their present value at the time of trial. Generally speaking, in all cases other than those in which future damages will be incurred for losses realized over a very short period of time, the decision to retain an economist is appropriate.

In determining whether the hiring of an expert economist is cost-justified, plaintiff's counsel must recognize that an experienced and knowledgeable forensic economist creates an efficient and professional means to completely develop and communicate future damages, thus increasing the case's settlement or judgment value. Therefore, from a cost-benefit analysis, the forensic economist, if retained early and used appropriately, almost always increases the value of the claim significantly more than the expert's fees, producing a net benefit to the client.

B. Defense considerations

For defense counsel, two questions exist: (1) whether to retain a forensic economist for assistance in the defense of the personal injury action, and (2) whether to present the testimony of the defense economist at trial.

Often in the defense of a tort claim the determination of whether to retain an economist, and, if so, when, is directed by a sophisticated client, i.e., the defendant's insurer or a corporate defendant which is either self-insured or maintains control of its litigation costs and strategies. The decision of the defense team to retain a forensic economist for an evaluation of the plaintiff's future damage calculations often hinges on the plaintiff's decision to retain an economic expert, the identification of that expert, whether plaintiff's expert is an economist known for presenting a neutral evaluation of the damages, and the totality of the opinions expressed by plaintiff's economist. When the plaintiff's counsel presents a report from an economist which overstates the plaintiff's damages, the defense team may need its own economist to provide the data, analysis, and questions for an effective cross-examination of the plaintiff's expert during deposition or at trial, and to present negotiation points for settlement discussions.

Defense counsel's analysis of whether to have the defense economist testify at trial requires the determination of whether the presentation of that testimony will create a "floor" for the damages. In the defense of claims presenting substantial future damages, the judgment potential may be significantly impacted by nuances in the data and analysis, including inflationary rates for wages, fringe benefits, and household services, projected life expectancy, and employment participation by age, gender, and education. In such cases, the explanation of the difference in those nuances to a jury may not only reduce the potential verdict ranges, but may also provide the defense with credibility as being fair and presenting experts relying only on nationally recognized data, analysis techniques and standards. Defense credibility on these difficult-to-understand economic issues lends itself to credibility with other experts, fact witnesses, and issues.

2.2 Choosing Your Expert on Damages

Once plaintiff or defense counsel decides to use an expert on damages in a personal injury or wrongful death case, the determination must be made as to the type of person to be retained. Many disciplines have fields of study that touch upon the data or the types of analysis required to evaluate and present future damages, including accountants, actuaries, financial analysts, and academicians in each of these areas. However, none of these fields of study encompasses all of the areas of analysis needed to provide a comprehensive damage assessment. Further, many of these types of professionals spend the majority of their time in academic pursuits or their narrow practice specialties. Few of these professionals will have the breadth of experience and research background to enable a complete analysis of damage claims in personal injury litigation.

Economics is the academic area that is most appropriate to produce an expert with effective knowledge of the data in order to provide an analysis of damage factors. An economist is more likely to have knowledge on issues relevant to the analysis of lost earning capacity and other aspects of economic loss. The economist typically has studied and has available to him current and historical data related to interest rates, inflation rates, wage trends, productivity rates, fringe benefits, worklife expectancy, work force participation rates, personal consumption, and market factors acting on specific areas of our economy such as health care.

In selecting an appropriate economist to assist in the analysis of personal injury damages, trial counsel must first ascertain if the economist has a Ph.D. in the field of economics. Certainly there are many qualified economists with only a bachelor's or master's degree. However, when presenting the often-confusing economic testimony to a jury, the expert's credibility is enhanced with a doctoral degree. Not all potential experts in the field of economics who have a doctoral degree are appropriate litigation experts. While perhaps qualified to testify on matters relating to losses and damage calculations, many such persons will not have appropriate experience in the art and science of educating a jury on matters relating to what, in the common jurors' experience, will be difficult and arcane concepts. Thus, the most appropriate expert is one who is not only qualified by education, but also has the experience of testifying and explaining the analysis to jurors.

These experts are known as forensic economists and most will be affiliated with nationally recognized associations such as the National Association of Forensic Economics and write for peer-reviewed publications such as *The Journal of Forensic Economics*. In selecting a testifying expert one cannot underestimate the value of experience in explaining economic concepts to juries. Many experts in various fields work primarily for either the plaintiff or defense side of litigation. Because the study of economic losses requires a rigorous adherence to known economic data, factors, and analysis, the economic expert should be one who has applied the analysis for both plaintiff and defense interests on a neutral and consistent basis. Such an expert cannot be criticized as to analytical techniques if he employs them consistently whether retained by either the plaintiff or defendant. The best economic experts are those who can testify that they have previously worked for both plaintiff and defense interests in litigation; they consistently use the same analytical analysis, notwithstanding which side of the case has retained them; and they have applied this "neutral" analysis to the pending case. Potential experts who work only for the plaintiff or defense side are, of course, subject to cross-examination on this presumed bias.

In selecting any expert, including a forensic economist, trial counsel must consider whether to hire an expert who testifies rarely as opposed to one who testifies often. The former may be viewed as more of an academician and less of an advocate. The latter may be criticized as being more of an advocate. Trial counsel is thus benefited by hiring an economist who is (1) highly credentialed academically, (2) conforming to the standards of the National Association of Forensic Economics, (3) published extensively in the field, (4) experienced in teaching juries the elements of economics and damages, and (5) known to provide consistent, "neutral" evaluations for both plaintiffs and defendants.

A. *Daubert* considerations

Trial counsel must consider the effect of *Daubert v. Merrell Dow Pharmaceuticals, Inc.,* 509 U.S. 579, 113 S. Ct. 2786 (1993) and its progeny in the identification and use of a forensic economist. State courts have likewise focused on the qualification and analysis of experts, including forensic experts, in providing testimony at trial. See the attached CD for a summary of representative cases by federal and state jurisdictions addressing qualifications of economists and related experts.

In *Daubert*, the Supreme Court held that the "general acceptance test of *Frye v. United States*," (which had held that the principle upon which expert testimony is based must be generally accepted in the field in order to be admissible) was superseded by the Federal Rules of Evidence, and directed trial judges to act as "gatekeepers" to ensure that expert testimony was relevant and scientifically reliable. Although the Supreme Court stated "that many conditions will bear on the inquiry" and "the inquiry is a flexible one in court," the court listed four pertinent considerations including (1) whether the theory or technique in question can be (and has been) tested, (2) whether it has been subjected to peer review and publication, (3) its known or potential error rate and the existence or maintenance of standards controlling its operation, and (4) whether it has attracted widespread acceptance within a relevant scientific community. In *Kumho Tire Co. v. Carmichael*, 526 U.S. 137, 119 S. Ct. 1167 (1999), the Supreme Court clarified that the gatekeeping obligation of federal trial judges applies to all expert testimony, not just expert testimony based on scientific knowledge. Thus, the holding in *Daubert* applies not only to testimony based on scientific knowledge, but also to testimony based on technical or other specialized knowledge. Further, the court reiterated that the *Daubert* test is flexible, and although a judge may consider the factors set forth in the *Daubert* decision, the judge is not bound by those factors alone.

The importance of the expert's qualifications and the federal judge's role in her gatekeeping capacity are underscored by the deference paid by the appellate courts to the trial court's decision. In *General Electric Co. v. Joiner*, 522 U.S. 136, 118 S. Ct. 512 (1997), the Supreme Court held that the abuse of discretion is the proper standard of review of a federal district court's decision to admit or exclude expert scientific testimony at trial. Further, in *Weisgram v. Marley Co.*, 528 U.S. 440, 120 S. Ct. 1011 (2000), the Supreme Court held that Rule 50 of the Federal Rules of Civil Procedure permits an appellate court to direct entry of judgment as a matter of law when it determines that evidence was erroneously admitted at trial and the remaining evidence is insufficient to support the verdict. The Court held that since the expert testimony was the basis for the plaintiff's claim, and was held unreliable and inadmissible by the Court of Appeals, the cause of action was properly dismissed with no right of repeal.

A listing of representative cases from federal and state courts addressing the admissibility of the testimony of economic and related experts under *Daubert* and state court gatekeeping decisions are set forth in the enclosed CD.

2.3 The Use of a Forensic Economist in Litigation
A. When to hire the economist

Once counsel determines that the case presents sufficient damages to warrant the use of a forensic economist, counsel must determine when in the litigation process to retain the expert. Some lawyers may believe that they can wait to retain the economist until late in the litigation process to see if the case can be resolved early, thus saving the expense of hiring the expert and the internal cost of accumulating the data and doing the work necessary for the economist to prepare the economic damages report. Such thought fails to recognize that hiring an economist will, in most cases, enhance the damages analysis and presentation, and that to appropriately prepare for settlement discussions counsel needs to have the supporting economic data and present it in a concise and persuasive format.

The skilled forensic economist will assist in conceptualizing the damages, determining what types of data and historical information related to the injured party will be required for the analysis of the damages, and suggest other types of experts that may be necessary to develop the damages completely. Many experienced forensic economists will provide counsel with a checklist which details the nature of the documentation required for presentation of the claims. For example, the economist in a personal injury or wrongful death action, besides tax returns, will also require the attorney to obtain IRS 1099 forms, W-2 forms, fringe benefits paid by the employer for medical, dental, and eye care, employer retirement plan contributions, and projections of the nature, extent, and cost of future medical care. The forensic economist will ask the lawyer to determine the nature and extent of the household services previously provided by the injured party and the reduction in those services post-injury. The experienced forensic economist will guide the less experienced attorney in exploring all of the possible losses available for the particular claim as the economist, with years of experience in analyzing such claims, will be able to direct counsel as to what damages may exist, the facts necessary to develop those damages for trial, and the required analysis.

Upon the conclusion of the economist's analysis, the expert will typically be asked by plaintiff's counsel to prepare a report detailing the economic opinions. These reports will detail the data reviewed, the assumptions made by the expert, the calculations applied, and a summary of the results. Typically, the report will detail the sources of the relevant information, i.e., tax returns, letters from employers, depositions, statements from family members, detail the time period reviewed, and provide the basis for future damages for the injured person's remainder of her life, or her projected life in a wrongful death case.

B. Discovery

Meeting with the forensic economist prior to the discovery deposition provides an opportunity for counsel to further learn the nuances of the data and analysis to be in a position to explain the damages at trial. At the deposition, counsel may well learn the opposing party's strategy in terms of its selection of economic data, factors of emphasis or de-emphasis, and its economic assumptions, i.e., life expectancy, employment participation rate, and personal consumption. The deposition presents an opportunity to demonstrate that plaintiff's case is well thought out, complete, and conservative. Often, if the analysis by the forensic economist is complete, clear, and conservative or "neutral" in nature, and the economist is known for working for both plaintiff and defense lawyers in a consistent fashion, the defendant may not call a forensic economist. Thus, the deposition of plaintiff's expert allows the opportunity to impress the defendant's decision makers and enhance the prospects of a negotiated settlement.

When preparing for the deposition of the opponent's forensic economist, counsel must meet early with her own expert to understand the data, assumptions, and analysis set forth in the opposing expert's report. When opposing counsel has hired a less qualified expert or has performed a flawed analysis, the deposition allows the opportunity to establish the basis to limit or exclude her testimony under *Daubert* and related cases. See the cases cited in the attached CD for examples of expert exclusion due to lack of factual support or appropriate analysis.

C. Trial considerations for plaintiffs

At trial, the economist is called most often near the end of the plaintiff's presentation of damages. The forensic economist's role is to tie all of the damage factors and analysis together for the jury in a clear and concise presentation. The jury must be taught economic principles, as none will have a Ph.D. level education or interest in the field. Trial counsel must meet with the forensic economist well before the testimony to prepare the outline of questions and to prepare demonstrative exhibits, which will teach the jury difficult concepts including inflation impact on wages, fringe benefits, and household services, as well as inflation rates of specific markets such as medical equipment, supplies, and treatment. The expert should be prepared to teach the concept of present value reductions in those jurisdictions that require it. In wrongful death actions, the expert must explain personal consumption deductions where required. As part of the trial preparation, demonstrative exhibits must be created which will allow the jury to see in chart or graph form the economic analysis and therefore have a better opportunity to understand the concept being discussed in the testimony. Finally, the testimony of the forensic economist gives plaintiff's counsel the opportunity to put forth a summary exhibit of all of the damages with the monetary losses being totaled. This demonstrative can then be used in closing argument to remind the jury as to the conservative nature of your analysis and the total amount of damages sustained by the plaintiff.

D. Trial considerations for defendants

Using a defense forensic economist to testify at trial presents an issue of trial tactics. Often, presenting testimony by an economist is viewed by defense counsel as creating a floor for the plaintiff's damages. Sometimes, the plaintiff's economic expert is so unqualified and/or the analysis so flawed that she must be attacked. Many defense counsels, having made that tactical decision, will present the economic testimony early in the defense presentation so that any testimony of potentially large damages is presented early, and allows defense counsel to then move to liability and other damage reduction issues.

E. Economist and related damage experts

As with the old saying with respect to computers, "garbage in, garbage out," the opinions of the economist are only as good as the data used in formulating her opinions. Much of the data upon which the forensic economist will rely will be obtained by the economist from sources traditionally used by such experts from the United States Department of Labor: nationally recognized inflation values, life tables, etc. However, economists are often attacked on cross-examination not on the information they developed, but rather on the information supplied to them by other witnesses, including experts, upon which they relied in formulating their opinions, for example, medical opinions with respect to the determination and duration of a medical disability. Experts in the area of vocational rehabilitation will review the injured party's work history, test the individual for vocational skills, and provide opinions with respect to the determination of a vocational loss or the diminution of the ability to earn income. In business litigation, accountants or financial analysts will often provide opinions with respect to the business' history of earnings, growth, and projected future profits.

All of these experts help to provide the information to the testifying forensic economist. The economist should be viewed as the "captain of the expert witness damages team." First, the forensic economist will be uniquely qualified among all of the experts to give an overview as to what elements are necessary to establish the economic loss. Second, the economist must have in his file and have documented all of the underlying facts, opinions, and assumptions upon which his report and testimony will be based. Thus, he is in the unique position among all of the experts to coordinate the acquisition of the information and to guide the attorney in what is required to be obtained to support the damages testimony.

For example, if an injured party is thought to have suffered a loss in the ability to earn income because of an injury which makes working more difficult, the economist will coordinate efforts with a vocational rehabilitation expert to test the individual, gain her present occupational abilities, obtain comparisons to abilities which the individual had in her previous occupation, determine what percentage of disabled people can find employment, and determine reductions in worklife expectancy. The economist can direct the vocational rehabilitation expert to obtain the required data to be used as a foundation for these damage opinions. Of course, the opinions of the related expert such as the physician, accountant, and vocational rehabilitation expert all must be introduced into evidence. If the testimony is not presented, the opinions of the economist may be attacked on cross-examination, including a *Daubert* challenge.

Accordingly, the trial lawyer must retain a forensic economist as early as possible in trial preparation. The experienced forensic economist will guide the trial attorney as what types of damages may be appropriate, the types of experts which may be helpful in establishing those damages, and the appropriate technical work performed by the related experts.

None of this can be done at the last minute. All of this work, when done early and in an organized fashion with a skilled and knowledgeable forensic economist, will benefit the client with an appropriate evaluation and explanation of the damages.

Chapter 3

Issues in the Estimation of Wage and Salary Losses

Frank Slesnick, Ph.D.

3.1 Introductory Issues

In most injury and death cases, it is necessary to estimate economic loss. Such losses are pecuniary in nature and can be measured using market-based values. This is the first of several chapters that will explain how economists estimate economic loss in these types of cases. We start out here with a discussion of how the economist estimates earnings loss. Later chapters will pick up other aspects of economic loss including fringe benefits, household services, and medical costs.

As discussed in Chapter 1, it is important that you provide certain information to the economist and that it be made available in a timely manner. You will need to supply earnings information that is specific to the plaintiff such as past wages, occupations held, letters revealing quality of work, and fringe benefits received. The economist, on the other hand, will utilize more general data such as trends in the economy, the future prospects of the occupation, worklife expectancy, and the types of promotions similarly situated individuals have received in the past. Experienced forensic economists will indicate what they need from the hiring law firm and what information they will obtain from their own sources.

As an example, Ms. Jackie Travis is twenty-eight years old and had worked for three years as a CPA for a large accounting firm prior to a work-disabling automobile accident. The economist will require detailed information such as where she went to school, how she performed in school, what were her current and past earnings, job performance ratings, and likely prospects for advance-ment. The economist will use his own data to examine the accounting profession, more broadly looking at general employment trends and chances of advancement into higher-level management positions. Of course, if the economist can narrow the general data further to, say, young accountants who did well in school and currently work for large accounting firms, so much the better.

If a report must be completed by a certain time, the economist ideally should be contacted several months prior to that date. (This may be less important if the economist is hired by the defense since the opposing side has already assembled most of the information.) The reason is that it takes time to assemble all the nec-essary data such as tax returns, a copy of Social Security earnings, or employer-provided benefits information. Further, it is not uncommon for an initial package of information to be sent to the economist and it is then discovered that more is required. A common question asked by defense attorneys of the plaintiff's economist is: "Was there any information that you could not obtain that might have made a difference in your calculations?" If the answer is yes, then their next question is: "Did you ask for that information?" Many economists have a laundry list of information they feel is necessary. If some is not available, they can at least indicate that the information was, in fact, requested.

A related point is that most experienced economists will be very reluctant to sign their name to any opinions that do not reflect adequate information. One of the phrases that are most feared by economists is: "I just need a quick and dirty calculation for purposes of the settlement conference coming up next week." If the economist signs her name to a "preliminary" report, any revised report will be compared to the preliminary report.

Finally, just as economists will be reluctant to calculate earnings loss based upon incomplete information, they are generally reluctant to calculate losses based upon hypotheticals provided by the attorney. The economist may be will-ing to incorporate a hypothetical from the attorney related to a legal interpreta-tion of a particular statute. As an example, in the Commonwealth of Kentucky many attorneys believe that discounting future losses is disallowed based upon an interpretation of case law. But some attorneys disagree and may request that the economist discount future losses. Economists may also accept a hypothetical if it is based upon the judgment of an individual with a different expertise. For example, the attorney may ask the economist to assume that a severely injured individual will live a normal life expectancy based upon the testimony of a physi-cian. As pointed out in Chapter 1 in the discussion of ethics, such hypotheticals must be clearly labeled as such. Referring back to our Jackie Travis example, if the attorney asked the economist to assume that the plaintiff would have become a top-level manager at the law firm within ten years, it is quite likely that this request would be refused unless it was severely qualified. If the likelihood of advancing to a top manager position is one in a hundred, then proposing this possibility simply as a hypothetical scenario, even for the purposes of settlement, should be avoided. A good economist does not want to be in a position of explaining why he has made a calculation contrary to sound economics simply because the attorney asked him to do so.

This point reiterates the discussion above concerning case-specific and general economic data. The case-specific data may say that Jackie Travis was very bright and the accounting firm where she worked thought she had excellent prospects for advancement. But the general economic data may indicate that very few advance to the top either because of lack of talent, burnout, or just plain bad luck. Similarly, the plaintiff may testify that she intended to work until age seventy-five just like her father did. However, worklife tables may show that for an individual like Jackie, expected worklife is until age sixty-two and the chance of working until age seventy-five is less than 10 percent. Providing a range of losses based on alternative case-specific and general industry data might be an appropriate procedure.

The next section of this chapter will examine conceptual foundation for estimating lost earnings while the following section distinguishes between expected earnings and earning capacity. The next two sections examine the methods for estimating base earnings and the rate of earnings increase in the future. Other sections look at the question of how long an individual is expected to work and how future earnings are translated into today's dollars. The final section considers issues that are specific to the situation in which the defense hires an economist.

3.2 Conceptual Foundations for Estimating Lost Earnings

In personal injury and death cases, the proper measure of economic loss is the difference between what the individual would have earned had the injury not occurred minus the likely earnings given the injury. Thus, economic loss requires estimation of two streams of earnings—pre-injury and post-injury. In the case of a total and permanent disability, the post-injury stream of earnings would be zero. As an example, assume that Jack Johnson was earning $22 per hour prior to an injury and that, based upon the report of a vocational expert, he can now only earn $7 per hour in a low-level clerical job. If Jack can still work full-time, the earnings loss in the first year would be ($22/hour − $7/hour) * 2080 hours = $31,200. The initial loss may be even larger than this if Jack can no longer work full-time. Further, the economist or a vocational expert will have to estimate worklife for both pre- and post-injury earnings. It is also possible that the injury may have shortened Jack's worklife. (The impact of an injury on earnings and worklife is examined in Chapter 6.)

The conceptual foundation for estimating economic loss due to a tort is applicable to all cases. A death case is analyzed the same as an injury case except that post-injury earnings are zero. Of course, some injuries are so severe that post-injury earnings will also be zero. Further, death cases often have certain considerations that are not relevant for injury cases such as the consumption of the deceased. (See Chapter 8.) Nevertheless, the models estimating loss for injury and death cases are equivalent. Further, the model applies to other types of damages as well. For example, lost household services are estimated utilizing a model that forecasts two streams of future services—the value of household services prior to the injury and the value of household services given the injury. As was the case with earnings, each stream of services must consider the value of the services per hour, the number of hours provided per year, and the number of "worklife" years. As an example, an injury may change the kinds of services that can be performed and hence the value of such services per hour, the number of hours per year services can be performed, and the number of years the individual can be expected to continue providing the services. (See Chapter 5 for a discussion of household services.) Throughout this book, the same conceptual model will be applied to earnings, fringe benefits, household services, and even medical costs.

3.3 Distinction Between Expected Earnings and Earning Capacity

Section 3.2 of this chapter discussed expected earnings, or what the plaintiff is expected to earn both pre and post-injury. Some states require that the economic measure be "earning capacity" rather than expected earnings. There is little agreement among economists about how earning capacity is defined, but perhaps the simplest distinction is that expected earnings reflect what you think the individual will earn while earning capacity reflects what the individual could have earned. The problem is that there is often little evidence concerning what is the potential of an individual given she made every effort to earn as much as possible. Many economists, in fact, will only use the plaintiff's past earnings as a proxy for earning capacity on the assumption that to do otherwise is speculative and may appear as a technique for claiming a higher earnings loss. Nevertheless, the economist should know if earning capacity is a concept that must be considered. There are obviously some circumstances where previous earnings are a poor indicator of pre-injury earning capacity. For example, if John Smith had recently quit his job as an attorney and prior to an accident had indicated he wished to return to his former occupation, then estimating the earnings of an attorney is reasonable—at least as one possibility. Considering information beyond the history of past earnings is even more important when there is little or no work history such as a minor or a woman who has stayed home for several years raising a family. Another example is the case of a newly graduated college student who, pre-injury, worked in a series of part-time jobs up to the point of injury or death.

3.4 Determinants of Base Earnings

As noted above, the economist must estimate both pre- and post-injury earnings. Initial earnings from which future projections are made are called base earnings. This concept applies to both pre- and post-injury earnings.

When the plaintiff has a well-established occupation and has regularly worked a full-time job, then estimating base earnings is relatively easy. The economist will likely equate pre-injury base earnings to the most recent tax return just prior to the injury, assuming there is not a significant time lag between the date of injury and date of trial. If the individual's earnings history reveals a more erratic earnings pattern, the economist will have to determine why this has occurred. Did the individual suffer from periods of unemployment or withdrawal from the labor force? Was there a serious illness that caused the individual to miss significant periods of work? If so, is it likely that this illness would have affected her earnings in the future? Is there an historical pattern of working part-time rather than full-time? On the other hand, if earnings seem to be greater than what would be expected working full-time, did the individual have a second occupation? Work significant overtime? Thus, when past earnings are cyclical or erratic rather than smoothly increasing over time, the attorney must provide the economist with sufficient information to determine the reasons behind the pattern. Further, this information will often take some time to obtain.

Estimating pre-injury base earnings when there is no prior work history would seem more difficult compared to when the individual had experience in the labor force. In many situations, however, the opposite is true. An obvious example occurs when a minor is injured. In that case, the economist will require information specific to the individual in terms of family education, family income, and possibly the minor's academic record. But beyond these basic facts, the economist's calculation of economic loss, including base earnings, is usually derived from general economic data obtained primarily from government sources. The analysis is more complicated if the minor is older—perhaps already in college. In that case, you may have to provide more detailed data such as college transcripts, letters from college professors, and testimony concerning the plaintiff's interest in various occupations. Similarly, if the plaintiff was a housewife at the time of the injury but had intended to return to the labor force, you will need to supply the economist with more detailed information such as her prior occupational experience and her future intentions.

Finally, base post-injury earnings must also be estimated. Even if a physician has declared a person medically disabled, it is possible that the individual can obtain employment. A vocational rehabilitation expert determines such potential for employment. Unfortunately, historical data are often unavailable because the individual has often not re-entered the labor market at the time of the trial. It should be noted that the concept of earning capacity applies equally to both post-injury earnings as well as pre-injury earnings. A plaintiff has an obligation to mitigate economic loss, and this requires that the vocational expert estimate the earning capacity of the injured individual even if they have not worked since the injury. (See Chapter 6 for further details.)

3.5 Determinants of the Future Rate of Increase in Base Earnings

Once the economist has determined base earnings, the next step is to estimate the rate of increase in earnings over the time projected in the loss analysis. There are three factors that must be considered. First, wages rise due to inflation. Individuals must receive a pay raise at least equal to the rate of inflation or they will suffer a decline in their standard of living. Second, wages increase due to general productivity factors in the economy, industry, or firm. Together, they can be viewed as across-the-board factors—increases that most workers in a company would receive. As an example, everyone in Firm XYZ last year received a 4 percent pay raise. This pay raise was the sum of anticipated inflation equal to 3 percent and changes in productivity equal to 1 percent. However, some individuals in the company enjoy even higher pay raises due to promotions and advancements. This source is often called individual productivity or experience factors, or an age-earnings profile. Thus, Francis Jones may enjoy pay raises because he both gets across-the-board raises received by all employees and is a bright individual who is on the fast-track up the corporate ladder.

The simplest case occurs when the plaintiff has a well-established earnings record. The economist can usually directly utilize past earnings growth as a basis for projecting future earnings growth. There are, of course, many situations where additional information may be needed. For example, it may be reasonable to assume that the individual would have attained several job promotions in the future. Conversely, past wage increases may already have reflected prior job promotions but such promotions are unlikely to occur in the future. In those cases, you need to provide the economist with significant detail concerning the individual's wage history including wage rates, hours worked, and job titles. In addition, the economist should obtain likely job promotions and advancements reasonably certain to occur in the future. This process can be simplified if the economist provides a list of standard questions that are submitted to the individual's last employer.

When the individual has only a brief wage history, the economist will examine data from published studies. For example, if Jones is injured three years after becoming an accountant, you can only provide degrees earned, three years of wage history, and perhaps letters related to his job performance thus far. There is not sufficient data to establish an estimate of future across-the-board wage increases or likely future job promotions given just this information. The economist will forecast across-the-board pay raises based upon past and future earnings of accountants and perhaps data for broader sectors of the labor market. Individual promotions will be based upon the types of promotions earned by accountants in the past. For some professions, "typical" promotions can be obtained either through professional surveys or government data.

Finally, the case may relate to a minor with no earnings history. In that case, the economist will rely on data that relates education and earnings. Various government sources will allow the economist to forecast both across-the-board raises and promotions for an "average" individual who had obtained a certain level of education.

Based on the discussion thus far, it is clear that in cases where there is little or no wage history, most of the information will be gathered directly by the economist. This information will reflect the experience of the average individual possessing certain characteristics such as all males who have achieved a B.A. degree. Imposing more specific assumptions is usually a mistake. For example, even if Johnny Smith, five years old, has parents who are both cardiologists, it is not proper to assume that Johnny would also become a cardiologist. When there is a substantial wage history, however, you must provide as much detail as possible. It is from this past wage history that the economist will piece together a pattern that will be projected into the future.

The economist will, of course, estimate the rate of increase in earnings. However, there are reasonable limits to what these rates will be in most cases. In this chapter and in other chapters, the authors will outline what they believe are reasonable limits for various economic parameters. In terms of nominal across-the-board raises, a range of 3 percent to 5 percent should apply in most cases. (See, for example, the 2006 OASDI Trustees Report.) Of course it is easy to come up with certain occupations in certain time periods where the rate of increase in earnings was outside that range. But if the economist has forecast across-the-board raises outside that range, especially if the forecast is for a significant period of time, you might question him before he gets on the stand. If the economist forecasts real (inflation adjusted) across-the-board raises, a similar range would be 0 percent to 2 percent. It should be noted that some economists might prefer to forecast the increase in earnings in real rather than nominal terms for a very practical reason—namely, doing so avoids the forecast of eye-popping figures at the end of the worklife. For example, a person who earns $50,000 today and is expected to receive a 5 percent wage increase over the next forty years would earn $352,000 in the last year of work. However, if the rate of increase were expressed in real terms such as 2 percent, income would be only $110,401 in that last year.

The situation is different when examining pay raises related to individual productivity. In some occupations such as corporate management, the potential for promotions and advancements is significant. On the other hand, an assembly line worker may have little chance for advancement. Thus, productivity-related pay raises require more case-specific knowledge, so it is more difficult to generalize a range that is applicable to most cases. You just have to be careful that these productivity pay raises do not reflect undue optimism about the person's future. Not everyone makes it to the top.

3.6 Issues Related to Worklife

In addition to establishing a wages earnings base and the rate of increase in future earnings, the economist must forecast how many years the individual would have worked. There are circumstances where testimony from the individual is important concerning her intended age of retirement. But in most circumstances, economists utilize either standard worklife tables that examine expected worklife or actuarial adjustments for probabilities of life expectancy, unemployment and labor force participation rates where both approaches adjust for various factors such as gender, age, and level of education. Such tables will indicate the number of years the person is expected to remain in the labor force and the expected number of years until she permanently leaves the labor force.

As noted in a previous section, the law often makes a distinction between earnings and earning capacity. This concept is applicable not only in reference to earnings per year, but the number of years in the labor force. Just because a person leaves the labor force at, say, age sixty-three does not mean he could not work additional years if circumstances changed such as a financial crisis. In jurisdictions where earning capacity is relevant, economists may include additional years to the standard worklife tables. Examples include work until full Social Security benefits are received or the number of "healthy" years remaining. Reductions in worklife might be limited to involuntary reductions for death, disability, and unemployment, rather than voluntary reductions for education, retirement or child rearing.

Just as there are reasonable boundaries for estimating the increase in earnings, similar boundaries apply to estimating worklife. A good starting point is the worklife tables, which indicate the number of expected years in the labor force. However, there may be good reasons for projecting an additional alternative. First, the plaintiff may have a long history of continuous employment and that history would have likely been repeated in the future. This possibility may be of greatest importance for women since their estimated worklife is lower than for men. Another possibility is that as mentioned above, the economist may need to estimate the potential for number of years in the labor market rather than expected years. But even when it is reasonable to deviate from standard worklife tables, there are still ranges which it is unwise to exceed. A useful benchmark can be derived from one of the more popular worklife tables authored by Gary Skoog and James Ciecka (2001). The authors not only provide the average worklife given age, gender, and level of education, but the likelihood that worklife could be above a certain number of years. As an example, the mean worklife of a thirty-year-old male with a high school degree is 28.26 years. (See page 33 in Skoog and Ciecka.) However, the article also indicates that 25 percent of similarly situated individuals have a worklife equal to 33.35 or more years and 10 percent have a worklife equal to 37.27 or more years. Given these numbers, if the economist proposed an alternative worklife of, say, forty years (age seventy), the percentage of similarly situated individuals whose worklife is this number of years or greater is less than 10 percent. The Court may question whether such a high number is at all reasonable given such a small percentage who actually work that many years. As noted above, worklife tables omit consideration of voluntary withdrawals from the labor force and hence may not be consistent with the concept of earning capacity. Nevertheless, worklife, even adjusted for earning capacity, should be within the realm of possibility. The usefulness of the Skoog-Ciecka data is that the forensic economist can determine the possibility of a particular worklife occurring based on actual data.

3.7 Bringing Future Dollars Back to the Present—the Discount Rate Issue

Forecasting future earnings is only part of the story. Given that any compensation paid to the plaintiff will normally be given at the time of the trial, all future dollars must be converted into current dollars. If, for example, the economist has estimated that future lost earnings will be $30,000 in ten years, any compensation paid today would be less than $30,000. The reason is that money paid today could be invested for the next ten years earning interest. The basic question is how much money must be paid today so that in ten years the plaintiff would have $30,000 to compensate for the estimated loss? That depends, of course, on the interest rate that could be earned. The higher is the assumed interest rate, the less money that must be provided today. The assumed interest rate that converts future dollars to present dollars is also called the discount rate.

There are several basic factors that drive the estimation of interest rates. First, the higher the rate of inflation, the higher the market interest rate. This is similar to the argument concerning the rate of increase in earnings. Second, lenders also demand a rate above the rate of inflation so their investment provides them with a real or inflation-adjusted return. Third, interest rates are higher the longer the time to maturity. Finally, interest rates are higher if there is a risk of default.

You should inform the economist if there are any legal parameters that should be considered. For example, either statute or case law may require some fixed discount rate or a rate indexed to some well-known market rate such as Treasury bonds. In some states discounting may not even be allowed. Further, in most personal injury/death cases, the economist must focus on rates that reflect relatively low risk such as government bills, notes, and bonds.

Within these legal parameters, economists will choose the discount rate they think is appropriate. The discount rate is, however, an area where many economists disagree. The main areas of disagreement include what maturity should the interest rate reflect—e.g., short-term or long-term—and whether the rates should reflect some average of past rates, current rates, or a specific forecast of rates. Two economists may legitimately differ on all these points, and because of these differences arrive at very different estimates of economic loss.

It should be noted that many economists do not provide a separate estimate of the rate of increase in earnings and the discount rate but estimate what is known as the net discount rate. Specifically, the net discount rate is roughly equal to the discount rate minus the rate of increase in earnings. As an example, if the assumed discount rate is 5.5 percent and the rate of increase in earnings is 3.5 percent, the net discount rate is approximately 2 percent. The reason economists focus upon the net discount rate is that it is the difference between the discount rate and the rate of increase in earnings that is important, not the numbers themselves. Thus, if the economist in the above example had assumed the discount rate was 6.5 percent rather than 5.5 percent and the rate of increase in earnings was 4.5 percent rather than 3.5 percent, the difference would still be 2 percent and there would be no impact on the present value of the future loss.

There are forecasts of future interest rates and wage increases. Several surveys of forensic economists have been published in the last several years. (See Brookshire, Luthy, and Slesnick, 2004 and 2006.) In addition to the survey of forensic economists, forecasts can be found in government sources. See estimates provided in the 2006 OASDI Trustees Report and CBO Current Economic Projections. Of course, the net discount rate can change over time and forensic economists may alter their estimate. Economic parameters are not fixed in stone.

3.8 Some Comments Concerning Economists Hired By the Defense

Most of the comments thus far apply equally to whether the plaintiff's attorney or the attorney for the defense hires the economist. However, there are some considerations that are specific to the situation in which the economist is hired by the defense side.

An economist hired by the defense attorney may serve a number of roles. First, she may be hired as a consultant and not a named witness. Her role is to review the report written by the plaintiff's economist and provide questions for the deposition and/or court testimony. Second, she may be hired as a named witness but limit her analysis to a critique of the opposing economist's report. She may or may not provide a deposition and/or court testimony. Finally, she may be a named witness, critique the report of the plaintiff's economist, and provide her own calculation of economic loss. Which role is utilized is dependent upon a wide variety of factors related to the case in question.

If the economist is hired only as a consultant, then the attorney needs to provide all the information that was utilized by the plaintiff's economist in a timely manner prior to the deposition and trial testimony. For some economists, the role of consultant is preferred given they can freely discuss the issue with the hiring attorney through written or oral communication. Further, the economist will not have to be concerned about upcoming testimony, although there are situations where her presence in the courtroom will be requested.

If the economist is hired as a named expert witness but is not asked to provide any independent calculations, he may still be ordered to give a deposition and/or court testimony. Again, the economist will need all the information utilized by the plaintiff's attorney in the area of damages. Further, any communication between the economist and the attorney could be subject to disclosure. It should be noted that the plaintiff's attorney would likely ask the economist if he could give a "ballpark" figure. A typical question is: "Wouldn't you agree, Dr. Economist, that the wage losses are certainly at least $1 million?"

Finally, the economist may be asked to perform an independent calculation of economic loss. The common argument against this role is that the numbers put a "floor" on economic damages. There are a number of concerns that can arise in this situation. First, should the economist estimate damages for a certain type of loss—e.g., household services—when the plaintiff has not done so? Many economists believe that if the plaintiff's side has not estimated these damages, they have made a decision that such damages do not exist and it is not the job of the defense economist to contradict that judgment. Second, should the economist utilize an assumption that by itself will tend to increase estimated losses? An example is when the defense economist believes that the proper discount rate is lower than the rate utilized by the plaintiff's economist. The solution is less clear-cut compared to omission of an entire loss category. It may be difficult for the defense economist to use the higher 6 percent rate just because the plaintiff's economist thought that rate was proper—especially if the defense economist is on record supporting the 5 percent rate. Third, what happens if the defense economist requests information that was not utilized by the plaintiff's economist? As an example, the plaintiff's economist may have estimated fringe benefits based upon standard tables while the defense economist believes that benefits provided by the plaintiff's place of employment should have been examined. It may be necessary for the defense attorney to request this information from the employer. Again, this points out the importance of hiring the economist with sufficient lead time.

3.9 Final Comments

Further details of this topic are provided on the CD. There you will find a sample case that provides an example that demonstrates many of the issues we have discussed. In addition, there is a "Concluding Observations" section, which examines a number of different topics not explicitly discussed in the text. Its main focus is how the attorney can most effectively use the expert witness who estimates economic damages. There is a Q&A sample testimony of a plaintiff's economist. Finally, some references are provided which are related to the material in this chapter.

Chapter 4

Fringe Benefits Losses

James D. Rodgers, Ph.D.

4.1 Introduction

A worker's total compensation package will often include more than just money earnings. In most injury and death cases where an earnings loss or loss of earning capacity is estimated by the economic expert, an estimate is also made of the value of employer-provided fringe benefits. This chapter (and the accompanying CD material) discusses how economists estimate fringe benefit losses and attempt to provide trial lawyers with practical and useful information.

Firms offer fringe benefits to employees for several reasons. First, firms may be able to buy a product or service at a lower cost than employees would pay if they bought it on their own. Health insurance is an example. The firm may be able to insure workers for an average cost of $10,000 per employee, whereas the employee would need to spend $12,000 to purchase the same health insurance as an individual. Second, firms may offer benefits as a screening device to select certain kinds of workers. Suppose a firm wants to hire highly motivated college graduates who want to work a few years and then return to school for an M.B.A. degree. The firm may offer a pay package consisting of a reduced salary and a promise to pay tuition in an M.B.A. program. The third reason employers offer fringe benefits arises because the U.S. federal tax code provides an incentive to offer them because many benefits are not taxed as income to the employee.

4.2 Collecting Information Needed to Value Employer-Provided Fringe Benefits

You will want to collect for your economic expert information about (a) the type of fringe benefits that was provided by the person's employer at the time of the accident, (b) the cost to the employer of providing those fringe benefits, and, for some benefits not universally provided to all employees of the firm, (c) whether the employed individual chose to receive that benefit or not. Whether benefits not chosen at the time of accident should be valued as part of the loss or not depends on the specifics of the situation. For example, the availability of company-provided childcare never chosen prior to the accident might be used in the future after the employee's pregnant spouse has a baby or a "couch potato" employee decides to become active and use the company gym. Plaintiff's experts will want to know about (c) in order to be ready for criticism by the defense side if the value of any unused benefits is included as part of the losses. Defense experts will want that information as a possible place to focus criticism. If possible, provide to your economic expert copies of union contracts, or any booklet the employer distributes to employees giving details about the various benefits available and the employee's cost of participating. This booklet, especially if entitled a "Benefits Statement," may also contain information about the costs the employer bears for providing some or all benefits. In addition to booklets describing benefits, many firms like to tout the costs they incur to provide benefits to employees. Provide your expert any information the employing firm has distributed about the cost it incurs on behalf of workers to provide fringe benefits. For employees who have had to terminate employment due to an injury, most employers are required to offer the employee the opportunity to purchase health insurance benefits for eighteen months after ending employment under the Consolidated Omnibus Reconciliation Act (COBRA) of 1985. The firm's document showing the cost the employee must pay for COBRA coverage should be provided to your economist.

For adult individuals who were not employed at the time of the accident, your expert will want to assess the likely occupation that the person would have pursued, based either on the past employment history or plans at the time of the accident. If the injured person was planning to obtain a unionized job, then the relevant union contract should be supplied. Even if a specific job cannot be identified, the occupation and/or industry where the person is likely to have sought employment may be known. Data from the U.S. Department of Labor shown on the CD provide employer costs for fringe benefits in various broad occupational and industry groups. For young adults or children not yet in the labor force, the best information may be the average cost all employers incur to provide benefits, as presented in the data from the U.S. Department of Labor or the U.S. Chamber of Commerce, which is shown on the CD.

4.3 Types of Fringe Benefits and Their Relative Importance

Fringe benefits are complex and varied and may differ considerably from one worker to another. Self-employed workers by definition have no employer-paid benefits; on the other hand, employees who work for large private firms or the government usually have an extensive package of benefits. The specific types of fringe benefits an employee receives and their relative significance need to be investigated on a case-by-case basis. There are legally required benefits (coverage under Social Security and Medicare, workers' compensation and unemployment insurance), and voluntarily provided benefits in the form of insurance (for life, disability and medical care), retirement plans and other benefits (e.g., use of company gym, a company car, company day-care facilities) and perks (e.g., stock options). There are entire books written about different kinds of fringe benefits (e.g., pension plans, health insurance plans), and in this short chapter and accompanying CD, we can only hit some of the high points. The focus here will be on voluntarily provided benefits with some additional treatment of legally required benefits on the CD.

Usually, the most costly voluntary fringe benefit employers provide is insurance: life, disability, and health insurance, and the lion's share of insurance cost is for health insurance. The employee is likely to pay a portion of the cost of health insurance as a deduction from pay.

The next most costly benefit provided by employers is a retirement or pension plan. There are two basic types of pension plans: defined benefit and defined contribution. Defined benefit plans have a formula for calculating the retirement benefits a worker is eligible to receive upon retirement that makes the benefit depend on the worker's earnings and years of service with the firm. The plan also specifies the normal retirement age, whether early retirement is permitted, and, if so, the amount by which the pension payment is reduced for retiring before the normal retirement age. Workers as well as the firm may make contributions to the plan.

Defined contribution plans are plans whereby the worker can set aside savings for retirement on which income taxes are deferred. Each worker has a separate account showing the contributions (the worker's and the employer's) made to that account. Employers may make contributions to the worker's account whether the worker contributes or not (e.g., 1 percent of pay), and additional matching contributions may be made (e.g., $0.50 for each $1.00 contributed by the worker) up to some maximum allowed percentage (e.g., 4 percent of pay) that the worker is allowed to contribute. Unlike the situation for a defined benefit plan, there is a direct relationship between the firm's contributions on behalf of an employee and the value of the benefit the employee receives. The percentage of pay the employer contributes can be multiplied by the employee's earnings loss to determine the loss of benefits.

There has been a marked shift away from defined benefit plans and toward defined contribution plans over the past twenty-five years and the trend seems to be continuing. In addition, many companies (Verizon, Motorola, Hewlett-Packard and IBM are examples) with defined benefit plans have been "freezing" their plans either by locking out new employees from participating or by halting new enrollments *and* stopping the accrual of benefits to existing employees. This is a point that may be emphasized by the defense—that the terrific pension plan would not have continued.

4.4 Placing a Value on Fringe Benefits and Issues That Arise

When placing a value on lost money wages, the task is made easy by the fact that the quantity of dollars lost is also the value of that loss. On the other hand, many fringe benefits, such as health insurance, are provided "in-kind." A dollar value must be assigned to them to assess the value of the loss. Due to their in-kind nature, as well as their complexity and variety, an expert could spend more time endeavoring to value fringe benefits than the time spent estimating lost earnings, which are typically a much larger damage component in dollar terms. Hence, experts may take shortcuts. Plaintiff experts need to choose these shortcuts carefully, as they may provide the defense attorney with opportunities for challenging what the plaintiff's expert has done.

In a personal injury or wrongful termination case, it is the value of the lost benefit to the injured or terminated worker that needs to be measured. In a wrongful death case, it is usually the value of the lost benefit to the worker's survivors who are named in the wrongful death suit.

The typical approach by a forensic economist is to estimate the value a worker places on a fringe benefit by determining the cost of that benefit to the employer. Because workers do not purchase the benefits directly, like a loaf of bread, but rather get the benefit through their employment, it is not obvious that they value the benefits as much as the employer's cost for providing that benefit. However, because group rates are lower than individual rates for insurance and because fringe benefits are not taxed, it is reasonable to estimate the value of benefits to workers at employer cost in many situations. Also, remember that employers who offer benefits cut wages below what wages would have been in the absence of the benefits. If the benefits an employer offers are not worth very much to its workers, other firms would compete the workers away by offering higher wages instead of offering benefits the workers did not want. By this competitive process, it is likely that the benefits being offered by firms are benefits that the workers at those firms truly value.

Let us examine several situations and indicate the way in which the forensic economic expert goes about placing a value on lost fringe benefits.

4.5 Valuing Fringe Benefits When a Young Person Is Injured

In this situation, resort to statistical data may be necessary because there may be no employer at the time of the accident, or if there is an employer, it may not be reasonable to assume that the employer will remain the young person's place of work for life. If little or nothing is known about the young person's future occupation or industry, the forensic economic expert may choose to estimate the value of benefits using government data on employer costs for all civilian workers, as presented in the CD to this chapter.

The first issue the economic expert will address is which benefits to include. Paid leave and supplemental pay should be excluded to avoid double counting— to the extent that such payments are already included in the statistical earnings data that the expert has used to project lost money earnings. Benefits for insurance and retirement pensions will very likely be chosen as the key components of benefit loss if the person in question is projected to be a worker with more or less average pay. The inclusion of the employer contribution for some Social Security and Medicare is controversial. Unemployment and workers' compensation may be included, depending on whether and how the negative contingencies of unemployment and disability are taken into account in projecting the loss of money earnings.

The general approach to valuing fringe benefits of a young person with little or no work history is to use statistical data on the average cost of benefits to employers, such as those shown in Table 1 of the CD, to derive a fringe benefit percentage. This percentage is multiplied by the estimate of lost earnings to derive a dollar value for the fringe benefit loss. Let us assume that the estimate of lost earnings has incorporated allowances for the negative contingencies represented by the probabilities of death, disability, and unemployment. It is necessary to make this assumption in order to avoid another double-counting problem. If future earnings are not reduced for the probability of disability and unemployment, then implicitly the assumption is made that the probabilities of disability and unemployment are zero. In that event, it would not be appropriate to include disability insurance, workers' compensation, or unemployment compensation costs incurred by employers in the computation of the fringe benefit percentage. The reason is that the benefits these payments are designed to provide to the worker have already been included in the earnings estimate because it has not been reduced to allow for these negative contingencies. Use of worklife expectancy statistics to project the length of working life is one way of incorporating the negative contingencies of death and disability. However, using a worklife expectancy does not take into account the negative contingency of unemployment. The forensic economic expert must make another explicit adjustment for unemployment. An alternative approach to using worklife expectancy statistics is to make an explicit adjustment for the probability of death, disability, and unemployment in each year out to an age beyond which the worker has only a miniscule probability of being in the labor force. The projected earnings for each year are then adjusted downward for the negative contingencies of death, disability, and unemployment. Then either (a) the fringe benefit percentage can include employer paid premiums for unemployment, workers' compensation, and disability insurance, or (b) expected unemployment compensation, workers' compensation and disability payments can be added to the earnings stream. Obviously (a) and (b) are alternatives and doing both would be double counting.

Now we are ready to compute the fringe benefit percentage. This can be done using the average wage and benefit cost data shown on the CD. The first step is to determine the base hourly wage to be used in the calculation. Because the earnings data that are typically used to estimate lifetime earnings include paid leave and supplemental pay, the appropriate earnings base should include all money earnings, including wages and salaries, paid leave, and supplemental pay. In June of 2006, for all civilian workers in the U.S. economy, this inclusive measure of money earnings was $21.35 per hour.

The next step is to determine the cost of benefits. This cost will normally be the employer cost incurred for health, life and disability insurance, plus the amount for retirement and savings, plus the amounts for federal and state unemployment insurance, plus the amount for workers' compensation. In June of 2006, the total employer cost for these various benefits was $4.00 per hour. The fringe benefit percentage is therefore computed as 100 x $4.00/$21.35 = 18.735 percent. The reason for excluding employer contributions (i.e., the employer's share of FICA taxes of 7.65 percent) for Social Security and Medicare is discussed in the numerical example on the CD.

The procedure recommended for estimating the value of benefits for young persons with no work experience is conservative in that it uses the employer's cost as a measure of the value of the benefit to the worker. Employers are able to purchase insurance for workers at a lower cost than the worker could buy the same quality of coverage as an individual. Furthermore, the employer provides the benefit as tax-free income in kind to the worker, whereas the worker as an individual would have to purchase the coverage using after-tax dollars. For personal injury cases, the post-accident situation may have another feature that makes the estimate of the value of health insurance too low. Because of the injury, the person may find that higher premiums must be paid for health and perhaps life insurance due to the greater health risk the person represents to insuring firms. While future medical costs due to the accident may be included in damages, the injured person may be more susceptible to additional health problems that make health insurance more expensive or impossible to purchase. A plaintiff attorney might choose to briefly explore such understatements of loss.

4.6 Valuing Fringe Benefits When an Employed Person Is Injured

Computation of the value of lost fringe benefits when an employed person is injured begins by determining the nature of the benefits provided by the employer, and using one or more information sources described above to assess the cost the employer incurs to provide those benefits. Every situation must be evaluated for its own special circumstances and peculiarities. For example, while it is unusual, a worker may be provided with a company car that can also be put to personal use, and the value of this benefit could be substantial.

After determining the specific fringe benefits made available to the worker, the utilization of these benefits by the worker needs to be assessed. For example, some workers are offered the opportunity to invest in a 401(k) retirement plan with an employer match at 50 cents per $1.00 contributed by the worker. However, the worker may choose not to contribute to the plan. As another example, a worker is offered the opportunity to be covered under the employer's health insurance plan, at a cost to the worker of $50.00 per month, but the worker chooses not to participate because he is covered under his wife's plan, offered at her place of employment. If the worker does not participate in an accessible benefit, then that fact needs to be taken into account. A benefit that is not chosen by the worker arguably has less value to the worker than would be ascribed if the worker did choose to participate in the benefit coverage. Adjustment for non-use must be made on a case-by-case basis.

Once the benefits are available and the worker's participation with respect to each of those benefits are known, it must be determined what benefits are lost and the value of those lost benefits to the worker. There may be a period after the injury but prior to termination from the employer when certain benefits, such as health insurance coverage, continue even though the worker has stopped receiving a paycheck for time worked. Care must be taken not to count a loss before it begins to occur. Then employer cost data can be used to project the loss of benefits, taking care to count as a loss only what the employer would have paid, excluding any costs paid by the employee.

Let's examine the two benefits that are typically the largest in dollar terms: health insurance and retirement benefits. Let us assume for purposes of this discussion that the injured person is rendered totally disabled by the injuries. If a residual ability to work remains and fringe benefits are provided by the jobs where the injured person is still able to work, those must be valued and deducted from the value of benefits in the pre-injury job in order to estimate the net loss of fringe benefits, just as would be done to arrive at the net loss of money earnings.

A. Health insurance

For an employed worker in a firm that offers health insurance to employees, it is preferable for the forensic economic expert to determine directly the dollar cost of the insurance that is paid by the firm as an estimate of the value of lost health insurance. Using instead a percentage of earnings derived from the U.S. Dept. of Labor or U.S. Chamber of Commerce studies may provide a poor estimate of what has been lost. This is because these data show an average that includes (a) workers not getting the benefit, (b) single workers getting the benefit, and (c) married workers getting the benefits for themselves and their families. Applying such an average for this diverse group of workers and circumstances will more likely miss the mark than hit it for a particular worker. A further source of variation for married workers with working spouses is that health coverage may be selected by one of the spouses to cover the entire family, with coverage not being selected at the place of employment of the plaintiff or plaintiff's survivors. The cost of some benefits, such as health insurance of a given quality, does not vary with the level of pay. Another reason to use dollar costs of health insurance as paid by the employer is that percentages can lead one far astray. For workers with very low earnings, cost of health insurance as a percentage of pay will be very high; for workers with very high earnings, the cost of health insurance as a percentage of pay will be very low.

B. Retirement benefits

The method used to place a value on lost retirement benefits depends on the type of retirement plan offered, i.e., defined contribution and defined benefit plans. Within each of these broad categories, there is a wide variety of retirement and savings plans offered by employers. The forensic economic expert must collect information about the particulars of the plan or plans available to the injured person and the person's participation. The valuation of one type of defined contribution plan and one type of defined benefit plan is discussed for purposes of illustration.

For defined contribution plans, the loss can be readily computed as the percentage of earnings that the employer was contributing to the plan. For example, if an injured worker was contributing 4 percent of her money earnings to a 401(k) plan, with an employer match of 50 cents for each dollar the worker contributed, then the value of the 401(k) benefits lost would be computed as 2 percent of the earnings lost from not being able to work for this employer after the accident.

An injury that causes future earnings to be diminished causes a loss of future retirement benefits under a defined benefit plan whose formula makes future retirement benefits depend on the worker's earnings. The size of the loss depends on the details of the plan. The CD gives examples of how such losses may be computed.

4.7 Valuing Fringe Benefits When an Employed Person Is Killed

Many of the points, issues, and principles discussed above for personal injury damages carry over to wrongful death cases. The major difference in the estimation of lost fringe benefits is the change of focus, under most wrongful death statutes, from what the injured party has lost to what survivors have lost. Hence, when a person dies who was covered at work by health insurance and by a pension plan, how does that death change the value of the fringe benefits that accrue to survivors? Another question about fringe benefits arises in death cases because it is typical in many states for a deduction from the loss of earnings to be made for the decedent's personal consumption or personal maintenance. The availability of an employer-funded health insurance and pension plan can change the spending pattern of the household and affect the deduction for personal consumption.

In regard to the impact of a death on survivor losses of benefits, let us consider health insurance and retirement plans in turn. Death of a covered worker is a qualifying event under COBRA that triggers the requirement that the employer offer continuation coverage to the decedent's spouse and dependent children. The premium for continuation coverage may be lower because the coverage is for one less person (the decedent) than was being provided before the employee's death. In any event the premium for COBRA coverage provides a good estimate of the value of the benefit the family has lost. After the end of the eighteen-month continuation period, the dependents have to go into the private market place for health insurance coverage. The cost of an equivalent plan in that market place gives an estimate of the value of the loss thereafter. If the decedent's spouse is also employed, then the loss may be mitigated by seeking coverage under the plan at the spouse's work, if one is available. However, the amount of mitigation depends on the specifics of the situation.

In regard to pension, again a distinction must be made between defined benefit and defined contribution plans. The loss of the latter is computed in the same way in a death case as in an injury case, i.e., as a percentage of the lost earnings. With a defined benefit plan, a lot depends on the details of the plan. Some plans provide for a death benefit if the employee dies before the age of retirement. For example, the Pennsylvania State Employees Retirement System has a provision for a death benefit. The amount of the death benefit is essentially the present value of future retirement benefits. The death of an employee in state service "activates" this death benefit. Some forensic economists regard such an activation of benefits as a reason to ignore a loss computation because the activated benefit is as large as the benefit that the surviving spouse would have received if the employee had not died. However, "activated" benefits may be considered as a collateral source and ignored, meaning that the economic expert could include the loss of future pension benefits as an element of damages in spite of the death benefit. You will need to advise your expert about the relevant statute or case law that controls this matter.

Chapter 5

Household Services Losses

Kurt V. Krueger, Ph.D. and John D. Hancock, Ph.D.

5.1 Introduction

This chapter focuses on "services" as a compensable loss due to personal injury or wrongful death. Services are the unpaid, time-based activities that people perform to increase their own welfare or the welfare of others. Service loss damages are usually calculated by multiplying hours of lost services by an hourly replacement cost, often set to the wages earned by persons who perform service-type work as a part of their job. Examples of services are preparing food for self and family, shopping for clothes, or teaching a child to read—food preparation would likely be valued at a cook's wage, shopping could be valued at a store clerk's wage, and teaching could be valued at a teacher's assistant's wage.

Personal injury service losses derive from the unpaid, time-based activities of the plaintiff that are impacted by injury, while wrongful death service loss falls to those unpaid, time-based activities of the decedent that are lost by her survivors. Under the definition of services, any activity that occurs during paid compensation time cannot be a service loss (e.g., handling personal matters while at work), nor can a service loss be something that transcends time (e.g., emotionally caring for someone is not a service, but time spent attending to a person's care needs is a service).

In this chapter, we offer resources to help you develop evidence as to the value of plaintiffs' service losses and understand the service valuation process of economists. We begin by discussing the nature of service loss as being related to the impairment of the ability to work, a well-recognized component of pecuniary loss due to personal injury. Next, we present how to measure the value of service loss using information provided by the plaintiff and recognized statistical sources for service performance data. Before concluding, we point out resources for the attorney to turn to for more information on the loss of services as compensable tort damage.

5.2 The Nature of Service Loss

The nature of service loss lies within the plaintiff's inability to perform unpaid, time-based activities due to physical harm. Any physical inability of a plaintiff to perform services must necessarily mean a physical inability to work and labor. The physical inability to work and labor has long been established as a personal right and an economic damage when that right is impaired due to injury. Those arguing against or minimizing service losses fail to distinguish between the *value* of services and the personal *right*[1] to perform them (*Collier v. Sims*, 366 SW2d 499; Mo. App. Ct., 1963). Given that people spend more of their lifetime hours away from jobs that pay them wages, damages for injuries violating the legal right to perform services should be an integral part of every personal tort case.

Allowable pecuniary service losses identify with activity that is time-based and can be valued in the labor market. In a particular case, a service loss might be the time necessary to mow the plaintiff's yard (an activity lost by the plaintiff due to injury) with its value set to the cost to employ a landscape worker to mow the yard. While we often apply feelings or special care to our service activity time, service losses are not based on emotional activity. When reading to a child, a parent might experience an emotional attachment to the child and give the child special attention; nevertheless, the basic service activity is reading to the child for a measurable amount of time and replacement cost. In *Sea-land Services, Inc. v. Gaudet* (414 U.S. 573; U.S. Sup. Ct., 1974), the U.S. Supreme Court mentioned a variety of pecuniary and non-pecuniary loss items for wrongful death. Pecuniary losses were lost financial support and service losses including the loss of the decedent's assistance, attention, care, education, guidance, nurture, protection, and training—all of which require time to complete and can be valued by the wages earned by persons in the labor marketplace performing such activity as a part of their job. Non-pecuniary loss items included love, affection, companionship, society, comfort, loss of enjoyment of life, pain, suffering, mental anguish, grief, and emotional harm—none of which are unique to linear time use, nor do they have a measurable market wage equivalent. As you discover evidence of service loss from inventorying a plaintiff's pre- and post-injury activity and then transmit that information to the trier of fact, it is your responsibility to make sure that a bright line exists between the pecuniary service loss that is time-based and has measurable economic value with other life activities that transcend time and are based on emotion, thereby having no measurable labor market value. Unlike the determination of wage loss in an injury case where the vocational specialist or doctor defines the level of disability, the loss of ability to do services is often self-declared and must be supported by the plaintiff and family.

5.3 Methods of Inventorying Service Loss

Many attorneys limit their evidence of service loss to a few obvious post-injury household chores that their client is completely incapable of performing such as mowing the yard, performing fine needlework, or getting down on hands and knees to scrub a bathtub. As a plaintiff's attorney, when you focus only on those activities that are a complete loss, you run the risk of missing important service losses that reduce the well-being of your client. The best way to avoid such omissions is to have a structured method of inventorying service losses. In a personal injury case, the inventory of service loss is related to services the plaintiff can no longer perform with the same ability as he did before the injury. In a wrongful death case, the inventory of service loss is not related to the total services performed by the decedent, but to the services the decedent provided to his survivors. For example, doing laundry could be a complete service loss to a personal injury plaintiff, but only a 60 percent loss to a surviving husband because 40 percent of the wife's laundry work was for her own clothes washing and ironing. While the total hours of household service work performed by a decedent are usually identifiable with a recollection of the survivors of the typical weekday and weekend activities of the decedent, splitting the work performed between hours only beneficial to survivors and hours only beneficial to the decedent is difficult and sometimes impossible.

The two common methods used to inventory service loss time are through "direct questions" and "time-diary." In the direct question approach, you suggest a service activity such as cooking, and the plaintiff recalls the total weekly time they devoted to cooking before their injury and how much time they now spend cooking after the injury. The plaintiff can answer with more, fewer, or the same number of weekly hours pre- and post-injury. With more hours performed post-injury, follow-up questioning becomes necessary to find out why there are more post-injury hours. Is it because the plaintiff has more hours to devote to the service activity since she is no longer working, or because her efficiency has fallen, or both, or neither and something else? With the same number of hours performed post-injury, the immediate follow-up question is: "so, your injury does not impact your time spent at cooking?" If the plaintiff responds "yes," the service loss of cooking is precluded. If the plaintiff answers "no," then additional questioning is necessary to discover services loss perhaps related to comparable hours before and after injury but post-injury at reduced efficiency or complication of service work.

A time-diary inventory approach to service loss has respondents record in time sequence their usual daily activities during a week, often splitting the week into weekdays and weekends. Instead of asking direct questions about specific activities, you ask the plaintiff to recount her typical pre-injury and post-injury day and then you count what you want to claim as service-related activity hours before and after the injury. For example, the plaintiff might state that before her injury on weekdays they woke at 5:00 A.M. and showered and dressed; woke the children at 6:00 A.M. and dressed and groomed them; cooked breakfast at 6:30 A.M. and fed the family breakfast at 7:00 A.M.; was out the door by 7:45 A.M. taking the children to school and then driving to work; worked from 8:30 A.M. to 3:00 P.M.; picked up the children from school at 3:30 P.M.; etc. etc.; and went to bed at 11:30 P.M. Post-injury, the situation might be to wake at 6:45 A.M.; talk to husband as he fixes family breakfast; go back to bed when family leaves to school and work; watch television before lunch; etc. etc.; and, go to bed at 9:30 P.M.. Once the complete typical diary is performed, you sum hours of service activity before and after the injury and then ask the plaintiff about any inconsistencies in her accounts or activities during non-typical days such as holidays or summertime when children are home from school.

Direct questions about service time often comprise typical service activities such as housework, food cooking and clean-up, taking care of pets, maintaining home and vehicles, household financial management, shopping, travel for household activities, and caring for or helping household members. After such lists are exhausted, the plaintiff is asked about any special services he used to perform regularly but now is no longer able to perform due to injury. Studies that compare time-diary to direct-question data find that direct questions typically produce higher time estimates than time-diary questions, especially for activities that occur frequently. For activities that occur infrequently, direct questions produce lower estimates, possibly because a longer period of recall is required. In general, the quality of both direct-question and time-diary measures is improved by the use of narrowly defined tasks. A direct question not narrowly defined is "How much time do you spend on housework in an average week?" It is challenging for a plaintiff to provide an accurate estimate to this question in a few short seconds of response time during a lengthy interview containing many other matters of recall. It is also expected that a respondent would interpret the definition of housework differently (e.g., does housework include washing the car?). As such, it is best to break up the direct questioning of service loss into a format that the plaintiff is comfortable with or simply listen to her recount services performance without specific questioning.

When interviewers ask persons a series of direct questions regarding their service time allocation, sometimes the sum of the responses exceeds twenty-four hours in a day. For example, many mothers report that they care for their children fourteen hours per day but they also report doing thirty-five hours of housework a week, fourteen weekly hours of cooking, ten weekly hours of laundry, six weekly hours of driving the children to school and extracurricular activities, five weekly hours of gardening and yard work, and two weekly hours of home and auto maintenance. Adding up the reported retrospective use of time reveals 170 hours of time use in a 168-hour week! While the mother may likely be near her children 98 hours per week, instead of child care being her primary activity, she might be doing housework, watching television, or relaxing. When asking a series of direct questions of service time, you should make sure that service hours are primary activities that leave enough time in the week for other activities including sleep, personal care, work, and leisure. When probing for service losses using the time-diary approach of "tell me about your typical day in a typical week," make sure the plaintiff does not leave out important blocks of time between activities. For example, there is obvious time lost to personal care and cooking between the consecutive activities of getting out of bed and eating breakfast. Again, as in direct questioning, make sure that overlapping hours of time use are properly accounted for and that time spent at activities including sleep, personal care, work, and leisure are adequately represented.

A third approach to discovering service losses is for plaintiffs to rate themselves in terms of efficiency and/or output of service effort before and after the injury. Plaintiffs sometimes feel more comfortable thinking about their aggregated service activities before and after injury and then giving a percentage reduction in ability to perform services. Once a rating of service performance is obtained, academic surveyed data regarding hours of service performance of people independent of litigation is applied to obtain hours of service loss. This approach has appeal in that a jury might not be able to fathom the daily life of the plaintiff before and after injury, but can understand reduced efficiency in usage of time especially after hearing medical testimony related to the physical impairment of the plaintiff. The other appeal of this approach rests somewhat in the confidence that by using litigation-independent figures of average service performance, the plaintiff is not over-reaching on service hours because compensation for loss is related to service hours claimed lost. As an example of the rating approach, a plaintiff might state that he performs less than half of the services he used to perform pre-injury. If persons comparable to the plaintiff in age, gender, work, and marital status perform eighteen weekly hours of services, then the plaintiff's 50 percent loss claim results in nine weekly hours of loss from the average. An important part of having plaintiffs rate themselves on ability to perform services is ensuring that the plaintiff can provide examples of how he arrived at that service loss percentage. For example, post-injury a wife could still do some cooking, but she does not have the energy to cook large family meals on Sundays, holidays, birthdays, etc. which represented 20 percent of her pre-injury cooking time; or, pre-injury she shopped six hours a week across town to find the best values for her family, but post-injury she must limit her shopping to two hours a week at a nearby mall that does not always have good prices or selection. In both of these examples, a percentage loss can make sense and possibly directly translate to other service losses that the plaintiff performed infrequently pre-injury but has post-injury limitations comparable to the examples mentioned and rated.

5.4 Resources Related to Service Loss

Since the plaintiff has but one opportunity to recover for lost services, lifetime projections of service loss are necessary with discounting to present value at the time of trial. Computing present value requires projecting an expected growth in the hourly cost of replacing services in the future along with an appropriate interest rate to compute present value of future amounts. At the time of trial, the plaintiff is at a certain age, with or without children, working a certain number of hours, etc. Ten years after the trial the children could be grown and hours employed could increase, with both events lowering service performance from the service hour level at the time of the trial. To evaluate a lifetime loss it is useful to reference academic studies depicting lifetime activity in varying household situations. On the compact disc accompanying this text, we provide citations and example data from several such studies that are often used in evaluating the plaintiff's lifetime service loss claim based upon the activities of others.

Because service losses are required to be stated at their expected lifetime value, considerations of the plaintiff's future mortality and morbidity probabilities are also useful in evaluating the expected length of loss. It is common to use mortality reductions such as the annual probability of death computed from life tables accompanied by some morbidity adjustment such as annual disability days or loss of function with advancing age to account for the expected reductions in ability to perform services in the future. To account for morbidity present late in life, the calculation of service loss is often truncated at several years before life expectancy. On the compact disc accompanying this text, we provide citations and an example service loss report that relies on mortality and morbidity studies that are often used in evaluating the plaintiff's lifetime service loss claim based upon the mortality and health status of others.

5.5 Conclusion

When framing a service loss claim, it is important to limit damages to those unpaid, time-based activities that people perform to increase their own welfare or the welfare of others. Service losses cannot be emotional in nature because they must correspond to a physical inability to work and labor that has long been established as a personal right and a measurable economic damage when that right is impaired due to injury. We presented the three common methods to inventory or determine service losses (direct questions, time diary, and efficiency rating) and the market replacement cost valuation approach with appropriate adjustments to compute expected present value. We provided caution that the plaintiff be careful not to overlap service performance hours with other activities or leave out infrequent, but important, impacts that injury has on her service performance. Following these simple guidelines, the plaintiff or defense attorney should be able to present cohesive service loss evidence for use in her litigation case.

Endnote

1. For example, the law provides to us a legal right to engage in our own meaningful life activities and tort liability provides to us a broad range of damages to compensate us "fairly for injuries caused by the violation of (our) legal rights." *Carey v. Piphus* 435 U.S. 247, 257 (U.S. Sup. Ct., 1978).

Chapter 6

The Vocational/Rehabilitation Expert

Robert H. Taylor M.A., L.P.C., C.R.C., C.D.M.S., C.L.C.P.

6.1 Introduction

The purpose of this chapter is to provide an introduction to the role of the vocational rehabilitation expert as an interface with both a life care planner and forensic economist. The role and function of a vocational rehabilitation expert, required educational and professional background, and standards of practice will be discussed. Case examples on the CD will be used to illustrate the role of the vocational rehabilitation expert in cases involving civil litigation.

6.2 Defining a Vocational Rehabilitation Expert

A vocational rehabilitation expert is an individual who, by virtue of education, training, and credentialing, is qualified to evaluate the ability of an individual to work and earn wages prior to an event and afterwards. The key distinction to be drawn here is the word "ability"—its meaning within the context of statute and case law and the distinction that must be made from "earnings."

A vocational rehabilitation expert historically has been an individual with a graduate degree in a specific vocational field, preferably rehabilitation counseling, awarded by an institution that is accredited by the Council on Rehabilitation

Education (CORE). Historically, the "gold standard" for vocational rehabilitation experts has been the master's degree. In recent years, doctoral degrees in rehabilitation counseling and other fields of rehabilitation have been developed.

The vocational rehabilitation expert has historically been employed in venues where the essential functions of the job have required him to evaluate the ability of an individual to work, identify the skills possessed by the individual for employment and aptitudes that he possesses which permit him to receive further training ultimately leading to employment, and effectively place such individuals in the competitive labor market. Many vocational rehabilitation experts now retained on cases involving civil litigation have been employed in traditional, nonprofit rehabilitation settings where they provided services to individuals with a variety of disabilities. Such settings would include those that provide service to individuals with mental and physical disabilities.

In the mid-1970s, a major expansion in employment opportunities for vocational rehabilitation experts occurred in the State of California. California Labor Code Section 139.5 was established to provide mandatory vocational rehabilitation services to industrially injured workers who were found to be unable to return to work at their usual and customary occupations. A number of states adopted the California model and the role of rehabilitation counselors in the private sector became widely recognized. Attorneys representing both plaintiffs and defendants in civil litigation became increasingly aware of the role that vocational rehabilitation experts played in evaluating damages related to lost wages and future earning capacity. Since then, vocational rehabilitation experts have been widely used in cases across the United States and other countries, as well.

It is common in civil litigation to refer to vocational rehabilitation experts as "vocational experts." A simple WESTLAW search shows that parties have relied upon vocational experts in more than 10,000 reported cases alone. As many of those cases make clear, vocational experts' testimony is often crucial to the trier of fact's ability to make an informed decision regarding the impact of the defendant's conduct on the plaintiff's earning capacity, and ultimately to determine the amount of economic damages to be awarded in the case. In most cases, vocational rehabilitation experts are the only experts qualified to give opinions about a plaintiff's employability and earning capacity.

There are many venues in which vocational experts have been found to offer expert opinions. The Social Security Administration has historically relied upon the vocational experts to assist judges at the Office of Hearings and Appeals to determine whether an applicant for Social Security Disability Income Benefits is employable within the meaning of the Social Security regulations. In workers' compensation cases, vocational rehabilitation experts also address the issue of employability as well as earning capacity in accordance with individual state statutes and case law. Long-term disability (LTD) policies contain provisions that require an assessment of an individual's ability to perform the essential functions of her own occupation or other employment consistent with policy language and case law. The only individual qualified to make this determination is the vocational rehabilitation expert.

This chapter, however, will focus on the role of a vocational rehabilitation expert in civil litigation and the role that expert plays. A discussion of the process involving vocational rehabilitation experts will now be provided.

6.3 Vocational Rehabilitation Expert Credentials

The gold standard for vocational rehabilitation experts has to start with the Certified Rehabilitation Counselor (CRC) credential. Awarded by the Commission on Rehabilitation Counselor Certification, the requirements for this credential consist of a combination of education and work experience. Education is typically at a core-accredited institution as discussed previously; work experience must be germane to the practice of rehabilitation and counseling, including the measurement of academic levels of achievement, aptitudes, and interests, and understanding the impact of medical and mental conditions on one's ability to work.

The choice of a vocational expert in any case that requires evaluation of ability to work should require, at minimum, a master's degree in a rehabilitation-related area, the CRC, and other credentials as discussed herein. Work experience is, of course, a critical variable that should assist the attorney in identifying the appropriate expert. For instance, if the vocational rehabilitation expert has no experience evaluating survivors of traumatic brain injury and their ability to work, as qualified as he may be, the attorney might be better off looking elsewhere for such an expert.

6.4 Methodology and Process Utilized by Vocational Rehabilitation Experts

Prior to *Daubert v. Merrill Dow Pharmaceuticals* and *Kumho Tire v. Carmichael*, vocational rehabilitation experts relied upon their core background, training, and experience in the development of opinions concerning an individual's ability to work and the lost wages and extent of lost earning capacity that this individual may have sustained. *Daubert* created the need to demonstrate a formal methodology used by the vocational rehabilitation expert to render his opinions; *GE v. Joiner* and *Kumho* refined the requirement for expert witness opinion in the United States District Courts. Many states have gone on to adopt the *Daubert* or *Kumho* standard for expert witness opinion at the state court level; however, most states still require the expert to merely meet the standard as set forth in *Frye v. United States*, a 1921 case with a much lower burden of proof.

The vocational rehabilitation expert was traditionally concerned with understanding how one's functional limitations of a mental and/or physical nature impacted one's ability to work. It would be common to identify the work history of the individual and, utilizing resource publications such as the *Dictionary of Occupational Titles, Guide for Occupational Exploration, Revised Handbook for Analyzing Jobs,* and all U.S. Department of Labor publications, identify how worker traits impacted on their ability to work. One treatise, for example, identifies the basic means of data collection historically used by the vocational rehabilitation expert as follows:

1. **Intellectual and Aptitude Functioning:** obtained from educational records review, interview information and self-description, and intelligence and academic testing
2. **Emotional Functioning:** obtained from verified work history, interview information and self-description, and personality assessment
3. **Interest Exploration:** obtained from personal interview, review of work history, leisure time activities, and standardized inventories
4. **Functioning in Particular Areas of Employability and Placeability:** obtained from job readiness inventories, personal interview, prior work experiences, and interview information (Parker and Szymanski, *Rehabilitation Counseling: Basics and Beyond,* (PRO-ED 1992))

Of course, the vocational rehabilitation expert would need to rely upon medical information that sets forth the individual's functional limitations to perform work-related activity. The vocational rehabilitation expert is not concerned with permanent impairment as this is a medical determination (*AMA Guides,* 5th Edition). Disability, that is, earning capacity disability, is a measurement left for the vocational rehabilitation expert to determine. The bridge between impairment and disability or the functional limitations that one possesses is assigned by the treating or evaluating physician. These limitations, such as "no repetitive lifting over 20 pounds, no repetitive bending or stooping, and no reaching overhead," all have distinct meanings for the vocational rehabilitation expert. Utilizing the treatises discussed above and other research tools, the vocational rehabilitation expert can determine what jobs exist in the competitive labor market that are compatible with these limitations. Only then, when the wages assigned to each job to which the individual is qualified by virtue of these factors is determined, can there be a measurement as to whether a loss of earning capacity exists.

The most widely used methodology that vocational rehabilitation experts employ for evaluation of earning capacity, thanks to *Daubert* and its succeeding cases, is the RAPEL methodology. This method consists of five distinct variables:

Rehabilitation Plan
Determine the vocational rehabilitation plan based on the client's vocational and functional limitations, vocational strengths, emotional functioning, and cognitive capabilities. This may include testing, counseling, training fees, rehab technology, job analysis, job coaching, placement, and other means for increasing employment potential. Also consider reasonable accommodation. A life care plan may be needed for catastrophic injuries.

Access to the Labor Market
Determine the client's access to the labor market. Methods include computerized labor market access technology, transferability of skills (or worker trait) analysis, disability statistics, and experience. This may also represent the client's loss of choice and is particularly relevant if earnings potential is based on very few positions.

Placeability
This represents the likelihood that the client could be successfully placed in a job. This is where the "rubber meets the road." Consider the employment statistics for people with disabilities, employment data for the specific medical condition (if available), economic situation of the community (may include labor market survey or employer sampling), availability (not just experience) of jobs, and chosen occupations. Note that the client's attitude, personality, and other factors will influence the ultimate outcome.

Earning Capacity
Based on the above, what is the pre-incident capacity to earn compared to the post-incident capacity to earn? Methods include analysis of the specific job titles or class of jobs that a person could be engaged in pre- versus post-incident, the ability to be educated (sometimes useful for people with acquired brain injury and other injuries), family history for pediatric injuries, and computerized transferable skills analysis based on the individual's worker traits.

Special consideration applies to children, women with limited or no work history, people who chose to work below their capacity (e.g., highly-educated workers who are farmers), and military training.

Labor Force Participation
This represents the client's worklife expectancy. Determine the amount of time that is lost, if any, from the labor force as a result of the disability. Issues include

longer time to find employment, part-time versus full-time employment, medical treatment or follow-up, earlier retirement, etc. Display data using specific
dates or percentages, if possible. For example, an average of four hours a day
may represent a 50 percent loss. (Parker and Szymanski, *Rehabilitation Counseling: Basics and Beyond,* (PRO-ED 1992); Weed, Ph.D., R., and Field, Ph.D.,
T., *Rehabilitation Consultants Handbook,* (Revised, 1991, Elliott & Fitzpatrick,
Inc.)).

     Prior to the development of the RAPEL methodology, the approach to earn-
ing capacity evaluation by vocational rehabilitation experts was much less scientific and relied more on common sense, or lack of it. For instance, much has been
made of the use of computerized transferable skills analysis (TSA) or labor market access computer applications. The U.S. Department of Labor in the *Dictionary of Occupational Titles,* (DOT), last revised in 1991, with most jobs included
therein last analyzed in the 1970s, identifies 12,741 jobs that existed at that time
in the United States labor market. Unfortunately, the DOT has distinct limitations in today's labor market where technology has, in many cases, revamped job
descriptions and provided access to certain jobs that individuals with disabilities
might never have had due to the use of technology. It also identifies jobs that
no longer exist in the national economy as information-based technology has,
in many cases, replaced manufacturing and production as key labor market sectors. O*NET, developed in 1998 by the U.S. Department of Labor, provides an
interesting way of analyzing the requirements of jobs based on what worker traits
are "very important," "important," and "not important" (See O*NET Printout).
O*NET, however, is very much a "work-in-progress." There continues to be disagreement among various governmental entities in terms of the ultimate application of O*NET. One thing is certain, however: the *Dictionary of Occupational
Titles* will not be revised again, resulting in a greater emphasis on O*NET in the
future.

     One of the most common mistakes historically made by the vocational reha-
bilitation expert is to use as a starting point an analysis of complete labor market
access by an individual to all 12,741 jobs that exist in the labor market. Such
an assumption is inappropriate since it is highly improbable that one individual
possesses aptitudes that would allow him to perform the essential functions of
jobs that might range from a legal secretary to an astrophysicist or medical doctor. Still, there are vocational rehabilitation experts who insist that the use of the
Labor Market Access approach is appropriate. Such experts, when challenged in
court, quickly learn that such an opinion is simply unsupportable. These computerized TSA applications are also frequent sources of abuse by vocational rehabilitation experts. These applications allow for the almost indiscriminate as-

signment of a number of variables to illustrate an individual's ability in any of the areas specified in the application. A specific general education development (GED) level in the areas of math, reasoning, language, and reading can either demonstrate an individual's qualification for a job or lack of it for purposes of this application. Changing one specific digit anywhere in the fields can have drastic impact on either pre- or post-injury outcomes. For this reason, these applications such as *OASYS, Skilltran,* and *Lifestep* should be viewed as no more than tools to be used by the vocational rehabilitation expert.

6.5 Records Required for Vocational Rehabilitation Expert Evaluation

Following is a suggested list of records to be provided to vocational rehabilitation experts for an evaluation of pre- and post-injury earning capacity to occur:

- complaint;
- disclosure statements setting forth the facts of the case (if filed in the specific venue where the case is filed);
- plaintiff's answers to interrogatories;
- medical records (complete);
- employment records;
- income tax returns; and
- Social Security annual earnings statement.

Proper application of the RAPEL methodology requires that a number of "action steps" be taken to acquire the information necessary to carry out a complete evaluation of an individual's ability to work and her pre- and post-injury earning capacity. These are as follows:

1. Clinical interview with subject of analysis (where possible);
   Information is obtained in the following areas:
   a. Personal background
   b. Education
   c. Medical status (subjective complaints)
   d. Description of medical history from subject and correlation with objective findings as set forth in medical records
   e. Work history including a description of the essential functions, physical demands, earnings, method by which job was obtained, and reason(s) for leaving the job
   f. Hobbies and avocations

     g. Vocational aspirations and/or specific ideas held by the subject for
     returning to work, including occupational retraining

2. Vocational Test Battery—Administration of standardized tests to measure the
following:

     a. Academic levels of achievement
     b. Aptitudes
     c. Vocational interests and personal temperaments

3. Transferable Skills Analysis
Use of computer application/technology, background, training, and experience
of vocational rehabilitation counselor, and labor market information to determine
post-injury jobs for which the subject is suitable.

4. Use of empirical data to identify wage earning potential in jobs to which the
subject has post-injury labor market access and placeability.

5. Employer sampling (unlike *Labor Market Survey*) to obtain specific information from employers in a specific labor market if necessary to determine placeability.

6. Determination of labor force participation and worklife expectancy using empirical data and resource publications.

     While the RAPEL methodology requires a vocational rehabilitation ex-
pert to address worklife expectancy, it is not uncommon to defer to the forensic
economist for this determination since the forensic economist will ultimately be
charged with identifying the specific dollar value of the economic loss related
to lost wages and diminished earning capacity. It is, therefore, incumbent on
the vocational rehabilitation expert to communicate with the referral source and
forensic economist to determine whether an opinion in this subject area should
be included in the vocational rehabilitation expert's report. The vocational rehabilitation expert, however, *will* offer the opinion regarding labor force participation, since this is a function of the individual's capacity to work as influenced by
post-injury functional limitations imposed by a treating physician.

6.6 Pre-Injury versus Post-Injury Evaluation

The RAPEL methodology is very convenient for also evaluating pre-injury capacity to work. In fact, all variables that the RAPEL methodology identifies can
be used in the identification of pre-injury earning capacity with the exception of
the "R"; the use of the "Rehabilitation Plan" is, of course, a post-injury variable.
In certain cases, however, the "Rehabilitation Plan" variable may need to be
identified in the pre-injury labor market earning capacity analysis if the subject
had a pre-existing earning capacity disability, either due to developmental disability or prior injury resulting in permanent impairment. In other words, if the

subject of the analysis was found to have a learning disability during her school years that required services to be provided by an educational specialist, speech and language pathologist, psychologist, etc., the need for such services would not be called for in post-injury to enhance earning capacity (as might be set forth on a life care plan); the need for these services to obtain a specific level of pre-injury earning capacity should be acknowledged by a vocational rehabilitation expert.

The remaining four variables of the RAPEL methodology, therefore, should be used by the vocational rehabilitation expert to help clarify the subject's pre-injury capacity to work and earn wages. As will be discussed next, "earnings" are not always presumptive of "earning capacity."

In most cases, the vocational rehabilitation expert can offer two alternatives for the post-injury earning capacity of an individual. In the case of an individual who has demonstrated through past employment and/or the results of vocational testing that there is the probability that she could benefit from occupational retraining, vocational rehabilitation experts should project a specific occupational training that will enhance post-injury earning capacity. In this case, the vocational rehabilitation expert should include the name of a particular school or schools, costs of training, period of training, period of time to accomplish an effective job search upon completion of training or prior to completion, the date when the subject is expected to re-enter the workforce, and the wage that she should be able to receive upon re-entry. If the training program is expected to result in an enhancement of post-injury earning capacity due to promotional opportunities, this should also be identified as well as the wages that one would expect and the period of time before such promotional opportunities should be expected.

Unfortunately, not all plaintiffs are suitable candidates for occupational retraining. If pre-injury academic levels of achievement, aptitudes, and skills possessed through prior employment suggest that success at occupational training would be improbable, the vocational rehabilitation expert should only consider those jobs to which the individual has labor market access and placeability through direct placement. It might be necessary to include the cost of vocational rehabilitation services to assist an individual to return to work even in the absence of occupational retraining. In this case, a period of career exploration followed by job development activities, résumé preparation, job placement, and follow-up should be included in the report developed by the vocational rehabilitation expert unless a life care planner is also involved, in which case these services and costs can be captured within the scope of that document.

Success in occupational retraining is usually highly individualized and many plaintiffs may not be suitable candidates for occupational retraining even if the results of vocational training suggest they might be. The reasons why occupational retraining programs fail are usually the period of time that has elapsed since the individual has participated in an academic program, problems in adjusting to her disability, objections to being "the oldest person in the class," familial pressures to return to work if financial concerns are evident, and an exacerbation of the medical or mental condition arising from the accident. For all of these reasons, it is usually a good idea to include the costs of a vocational rehabilitation expert to provide oversight during the training program and, where possible, to actually provide such services.

6.7 Evaluation of Earning Capacity in Pediatric Cases

Just as RAPEL provides the methodology for evaluation of earning capacity in the adult with a work history, PEEDS-RAPEL© provides the means of evaluating the earning capacity of a child or individual without a formal work history (Neulicht and Berens, 2003) (Neulicht, A. and Berens, D., "The Role of a Vocational Counselor in Life Care Planning," *Pediatric Life Care Planning and Case Management*, CRC Press 2004).

PEEDS-RAPEL© first requires evaluation of the following prior to applying the RAPEL criteria discussed previously:

Parental/Family Occupations

Obtain family work history (occupations and skill levels), including information from parents, older siblings, aunts and uncles, grandparents, and adults who are likely to provide a role model for the child. Also include military experience, volunteer or community service, and vocational activities. Consider vocational assessment of parents, as appropriate, to determine a pattern of aptitudes or trait profile.

Educational Attainment

Establish family patterns of educational attainment including information from the immediate and extended family (as above). Determine not only the academic level and degrees earned, but also the skills obtained through education and training. Administer or coordinate referral for achievement and/or intellectual assessment of parents as needed.

Evaluation Results

Determine the child's functional capacities through interviews and formal assessment of physical, cognitive, emotional, and vocational capacity. Consider academic skills, interests, aptitudes, personality, assessment of independence and ADLs, and family patterns of hobbies and leisure activities. When appropriate, compare the pre-injury status and function.

Developmental Stage

Consider the normal developmental tasks of a particular age (e.g., ADLs, career development). Determine the effects of a disability on function and ability to achieve developmental milestones. Provide recommendations for remediation and accommodation to facilitate the maximum level of function for the child.

Synthesis

Integrate results of the interview, parent and family occupations, educational attainment, evaluation results, developmental stage, and opinions regarding functional capacities to determine the impact of the disability and likely options that are, within reasonable probability, available to the child.

While the forensic economic literature does contain other approaches in determining the earning capacity of a child or one without a vocational history, the above methodology does provide a unique framework for the vocational rehabilitation expert to address this subject. Such an evaluation is hardly speculative and, once sound vocational rehabilitation concepts are applied, a reliable method of predicting academic and vocational outcome for a child can readily be done. The forensic economist can then utilize this information to project economic losses arising from an alteration in what the pre-injury outcomes would have been.

6.8 Earnings versus Earnings Capacity

One of the most common mistakes made by attorneys on both sides of the bar when evaluating a claim for lost wages and lost earnings capacity is to assume that pre-injury earnings are presumptive of earnings capacity. While in some cases this is true, such as the worker with a thirty-year history of employment with a railroad or as a truck driver, the fact is, most workers do not have such tenure in their jobs. For this reason, it is incumbent upon the vocational rehabilitation expert to determine the probability that an individual's pre-injury earnings are, in fact, presumptive of their earnings capacity. In a case where an individual does not possess the necessary worker traits (such as the skills to perform the essential functions of the job of a business executive who is paid $100,000 a year, although that job was given to the individual by his father who owned the company), he would not be expected to earn that amount of money in the competitive labor market if forced to compete with other workers for that job. Therefore, in such a case, pre-injury earnings would probably not be presumptive of pre-injury earning capacity. Any such conclusions would probably lead to a strong rebuttal by opposing expert. This is not to say, however, that there are plaintiff attorneys and vocational rehabilitation experts they retained who would not proceed in such a manner. However, these would not be an example of an unbiased, objective evaluation considering all of the data available for review.

It would also be inappropriate in the case of a tenured college professor—who was taking a year off to write a treatise and who, during that period of time, decided to work as a courier part-time for his wife's travel agency when injured in a motor vehicle accident—to use his current wages as earning capacity, since the minimal wages his wife would probably have paid him, if he was paid at all, would not be comparable to what he would have been expected to earn as a tenured college professor. Sadly, however, I have seen vocational rehabilitation experts and forensic economists retained by the defendant in cases with similar facts who would argue that the low wages paid as a courier would be, in fact, presumptive of the earning capacity of the injured subject for reasons that only they can define. Sometimes the fault here lies with the retaining attorney not providing full and complete information to her experts; most often, however, it is the expert who chooses to be biased and not objective in her approach.

6.9 Evaluation of Individuals with Preexisting Earning Capacity Disabilities

It is invariably the approach of plaintiffs' attorneys to argue that the plaintiff was "whole" at the time of injury in the specific case. Although the history of prior injury or permanent impairment might not be suggestive of a pre-injury earning capacity disability, very often this is, in fact, the case, and should be considered by vocational rehabilitation experts and forensic economists regardless of what side retains them. This underscores the importance of obtaining a full and complete medical history from the plaintiff and obtaining detailed information with regard to history of prior industrial injuries, other injuries, and other medical conditions that may have existed prior to the subject accident. Such information may be identified simply by asking the plaintiff if he had ever sustained an industrial injury. Questions that follow very often will lead to disclosure of prior industrial injuries, resulting in a permanent impairment and functional limitations that would have a profound impact on their pre-injury wage earning capacity. Ultimately, this may impact the opinion as to whether or not earnings at the time of injury were presumptive of earning capacity.

The presence of pre-existing functional limitations may affect pre-injury labor market access, but have no impact on pre-injury earnings. The same conclusion can be reached with regard to post-injury functional limitations and earnings.

A case in point would involve a concert pianist who sustained a traumatic amputation of the tip of her fifth minor finger. For most workers such an injury, while of course resulting in permanent impairment, would probably not result in functional limitations resulting in an earning capacity disability. After all, most individuals would either still be able to perform all of the essential functions of their usual and customary job or could do so with the use of assistive technology such as, for instance, a one-handed keyboard, the cost of which is captured in a life care plan. With such technology, an individual, while perhaps losing labor market access and placeability to a specific job, could be expected to work in other jobs with no loss of earning power compared to what she would have been expected to earn, or did earn, pre-injury.

In the case of the concert pianist, however, it stands to reason that her days of playing in a concert setting would come to an end. In such a case, the loss of capacity to earn could certainly be reasonably demonstrated; however, whether this would result in measurable actual earnings loss would remain to be seen. If it could be demonstrated through research and the like that the concert pianist could earn an equivalent amount of money as a composer, conductor, instructor, or in other forms of work where the loss of the finger would not have an impact, there would be little basis for a conclusion that a measurable, tangible loss of *earnings* would occur in the future, although a loss of labor market access and placeability certainly would.

It stands to reason that the forensic economist would not have the prerequisite background, training, and experience to identify the other jobs in the alternative forms of employment available to the concert pianist; on the other hand, the vocational rehabilitation expert would.

A converse example of a severe injury demonstrates the impact on earning capacity depending on the pre-injury labor market access and placeability of a specific individual. A traumatic amputation of the major arm of a truck driver would preclude that individual from ever driving a truck competitively again. If the measure of this individual's academic levels of achievement and aptitudes demonstrates borderline intellectual functioning and insufficient aptitudes to engage in occupational retraining, the loss of earning capacity for such an individual would probably be as catastrophic as the loss of the extremity itself. If the individual were found to have the capacity for occupational retraining, the impact on earning capacity would be more limited.

An actual case that comes to mind involves a young man, twenty-one years of age, who sustained traumatic amputations to both upper extremities at the elbow in an electrocution. Pre-injury, this man was a high school dropout, was quite active with illegal substances, and had a very sporadic work history involving unskilled, minimum-wage jobs. Essentially, this man worked when he wanted to support his drug use and relied on friends for other sources of income. The injury occurred when, in a drunken stupor, he lifted a manhole cover and fell 20 feet below the street level where he wandered into an electrical transformer, was shocked, and sustained the amputations.

Following emergency medical treatment and ultimately being fitted with upper extremity prosthetics, this individual decided that this was his "wake-up call," returned to school, earned his GED and subsequently went on to receive post-secondary education and was gainfully employed as a computer draftsman. While certainly no one is suggesting that he is better off with the loss of his upper extremities, it can be predicted within reasonable vocational rehabilitation certainty that, but for the injury, his labor market placeability would have continued to be minimal with limited earnings potential. There were no factors in place in this man's life that would have indicated that a "turn-around" of his life would have occurred. Post-injury, he has skills that allow him to earn a solid living; he is in great demand and an inspiration to co-workers.

6.10 Post-Injury Earning Capacity Evaluation—What Information to Use?

A vocational rehabilitation expert frequently is met with conflicting information as to functional outcome. It is not uncommon in civil cases for the vocational rehabilitation expert to be faced with a dilemma: What functional limitations do I use for my evaluation? There is often a discrepancy between treating and consulting (evaluating) physicians who perform "Independent Medical Examinations" (IME) in terms of the injuries the subject sustained and the functional limitations she has as a result thereof. For instance, in the case of a back injury resulting in surgery to the lumbar disk, a treating orthopedist or neurosurgeon may determine that the individual has sustained a 10 percent permanent impairment of the whole person and has limitations of no repetitive bending, stooping, or lifting over 20 pounds. The IME physician on the other hand may find that the individual can lift up to 50 pounds without problem or, worse yet for the vocational rehabilitation expert, determine that the injured lumbar disk itself was not causally related to the accident in question.

When faced with such conflicting evidence, the vocational rehabilitation expert must rely on the codes of ethics of the credentialing entities from which he holds credentials and the professional associations of which he is a member. It would not be proper, therefore, for a vocational rehabilitation expert to assume that only one of the opinions is accurate. In other words, it would not be appropriate for the vocational rehabilitation expert to base her entire opinions on the findings of Dr. "X," who imposed a 20-pound weightlifting limitation. It would similarly be inappropriate for a vocational rehabilitation expert to rely upon the opinions of Dr. "Y" who imposed a 50-pound weight limit or Dr. "Z" who determined that the limitations possessed by the plaintiff were not the result of an injury sustained in the subject accident.

It would be appropriate for the vocational rehabilitation expert, however, to offer opinions indicating, "assuming that Dr. X's opinions are more probably correct, my opinion is _____, assuming Dr. Y's opinions are more probably correct, my opinions are _____," and if one were to assume that Dr. Z's opinions are more probably correct, the subject's capacity to work and earn wages is unchanged from pre-injury levels.

It is imperative to understand that the vocational rehabilitation expert is not a trier of fact. The trier of fact in any case in civil litigation is the entity that will ultimately render the decision, such as the judge or jury. A credible vocational rehabilitation expert (and this applies not only to vocational rehabilitation experts, but to all expert witnesses on damages in cases involving civil litigation) is the expert who assumes all facts given to him for consideration and bases his opinion on such facts.

Very often, however, the referring attorney may not provide all information to the vocational rehabilitation expert. If such is the case, the vocational rehabilitation expert must base her opinion on information provided for review. It is, in such cases, imperative that the following disclaimer be added at the end of the report: "The opinions contained herein are offered to a reasonable degree of vocational rehabilitation certainty and are subject to revision should additional information become available for review."

6.11 Barriers to Vocational Rehabilitation Evaluation

One of the most important things for a vocational rehabilitation expert to do when conducting an earning capacity evaluation is to meet with the subject of the analysis. In many venues, however, such an evaluation may not be possible, although this is allowed for cases venued in U.S. District Court.

In many states, for instance, the rule equivalent of Federal Rule 35 may not include the vocational rehabilitation expert as an individual to whom the plaintiff must present himself for purposes of examination. In many cases, attorneys are arguing under the equivalent of Rule 26 of the Federal Rules of Evidence that in order to evaluate a claim for damages, they are entitled to have the plaintiff examined by the expert most qualified to evaluate the specific area of damages. In cases involving claims for lost wages and lost earning capacity, that individual is the vocational rehabilitation expert. A case law in many states is conflicting as to whether or not a vocational rehabilitation expert is one of the qualifying experts to perform an in-person evaluation of the plaintiff.

I have often believed that a plaintiff attorney, however, who has a plaintiff with nothing to hide, will make the plaintiff available to an expert retained by the defendant without objection. After all, the plaintiff attorney will have had his client evaluated by a vocational rehabilitation expert of his choosing, so unless he is in the position of merely wanting to try to "gain the upper hand," it seems silly to preclude the defendants from having the vocational rehabilitation expert of their choosing do a similar evaluation. For this reason, I *always* ask my referring attorney, if he or she happens to be a defense attorney, to request that I have the opportunity to meet with the plaintiff. In cases where I am deprived of that opportunity, the report I do will reflect that the request was made, but plaintiff's counsel did not allow this.

The importance of this approach cannot be overstated. One of the most fruitful areas of cross-examination for a defense expert at deposition or trial revolves around the vocational rehabilitation expert's ability to interview the plaintiff, a task which no doubt had been carried out by her counterpart retained by the plaintiff. Failure to interview the plaintiff or request the ability to do so suggests to the triers of fact that that expert has not been as complete in her evaluation as the expert retained by the plaintiff. While this is, of course, very often not the case, perception at times becomes reality.

By requesting the opportunity to meet with the plaintiff, this also removes that very question from the plaintiff attorney's arsenal of questions at deposition or trial. If the opposing attorney chooses to ask that question, the response by the vocational rehabilitation expert retained by the defendant may be successful in suggesting to the jury that this attorney "has something to hide," and if he was not upfront enough to allow the plaintiff to meet with an opposing vocational rehabilitation expert, are there other areas of the case where plaintiff's counsel may either have misrepresented his case or perhaps not have been candid? Why has the jury taken away from its task at hand, to whit, to objectively review the evidence and reach a determination? All sides can be best served by allowing such an evaluation to go forth. It also stands to reason that such an evaluation will allow the defendants to more completely evaluate the case, thus perhaps leading to settlement as opposed to trial.

It is the nature of attorneys to be combative and they are, of course, advocates for their clients. An expert who is important to the case for both sides is the vocational rehabilitation expert. However, the expert should not be caught up in such disputes, since in the long run no side "wins" when expert witness opinion must rely upon facts and data that are less than could have been made available. This weakness in opinion often leads to even more disputes in the course of the litigation. As can be seen, however, the vocational rehabilitation expert does have some control over how he may choose to conduct his evaluation.

In cases where an in-person evaluation is simply not possible, the vocational rehabilitation expert does have options available to him. He may, for instance, ask to sit in on the deposition of the plaintiff. While he certainly could not ask questions, it is very important that he be able to observe what the plaintiff's response to questions are and learn first-hand about the individual's cognitive abilities insofar as information processing is concerned, as well as what verbal skills the plaintiff has. These determinations cannot always be made by reviewing a deposition transcript. The vocational rehabilitation expert retained by the plaintiff should, of course, have met with the plaintiff in person, and acquired some fund of information about the plaintiff's level of functioning in these areas.

Regardless of whether obtained by the plaintiff or defendant, the vocational rehabilitation expert should be expected to obtain a full and complete set of records, especially medical records. Since the basic foundation for determining residual functional capacity, that is the plaintiff's functional exertional capabilities considering the permanent impairment in functional limitations arising from the accident, is the backbone of the vocational rehabilitation expert's opinion, such information must be provided as completely as possible. Similarly, all records noted on the list of suggested records earlier in this chapter should also be provided to the vocational rehabilitation experts retained by both the plaintiff and defendant.

Like other professions, vocational rehabilitation experts, while now referred to as rehabilitation counselors, should be held accountable to perform their work as an expert in a manner expected of them as set forth by the bodies providing them with credentials and associations in which they hold membership. As discussed earlier, rehabilitation counselors typically hold the certified rehabilitation counselor (CRC) credential. This credential, awarded by the Commission on Rehabilitation Counselor Certification, sets forth the ethical conduct expected of a rehabilitation counselor and contains a specific section related to forensic evaluations. It is always a good idea for the retaining and opposing attorney to ask the expert whether she is subject to any codes of ethics in her profession and, if so, the last time she reviewed them. Similar codes of ethics exist for other credentials awarded to vocational rehabilitation counselors such as the certified disability management specialist (CDMS) credential, certified case manager (CCM) credential, certified life care planner (CLCP) credential and, of course, any credential she holds from a state licensing body. In addition, most rehabilitation counselors are members of professional associations. Most rehabilitation counselors who perform forensic work are members of the International Association of Rehabilitation Professionals (IARP). The IARP members are expected to comply with its standards of practice and code of professional ethics. This, too, has a specific section for forensic practice. The American Board of Vocational Experts (ABVE) is a credentialing body for vocational experts. While there have been questions raised by many about certain claims made by ABVE as to the value of its members' credentials, ABVE does have a code of ethics that its members are expected to abide by. The National Rehabilitation Association (NRA) and National Rehabilitation Counseling Association (NRCA) are other associations in which rehabilitation counselors may hold membership. These associations also have published codes of ethics with which its members are expected to comply.

6.12 Interface with Forensic Economists and other Experts

In determining post-injury earning capacity, a vocational rehabilitation expert may find that there is a need for occupational training, assistive technology, on-going medical treatment, medications, therapies, etc., in order for an individual to return to the competitive labor market. Many vocational rehabilitation experts are also accomplished life care planners and can, within the body of their report, identify these future care needs and develop a life plan. In some cases, the retaining attorney may have retained the life care planner to set forth these future care needs. If this occurs, it is essential for the vocational rehabilitation expert to communicate with the life care planner and make clear what he thinks the plaintiff requires in order to accomplish a return to work. It may also be that the vocational rehabilitation expert has a different opinion than the life care planner in terms of future functional outcome. It is very often difficult, not to mention problematic, for an attorney to have two experts offering conflicting opinions in terms of functional outcome. The life care planner may believe that the plaintiff requires assistance performing home-based activities and provide for a home health aide in the life care plan while the vocational rehabilitation expert has the same individual returning to work and being outside of the home at the time the life care planner expects the home care services to be provided. It is, therefore, critical for both the vocational rehabilitation counselor and life care planner to communicate and share their respective opinions. If conflicts occur, it falls to the attorney to discuss the case with both experts and, hopefully, develop a consensus rather than a division in the opinions to be provided to the forensic economist.

The report generated by the vocational rehabilitation expert should be clear and set forth opinions regarding both pre- and post-injury earning capacity. The forensic economist should be able to literally pick up and read the vocational rehabilitation expert's report, as well as that of the life care planner for that matter, and proceed with economic calculations using the reports of the vocational rehabilitation expert or life care planner as foundation.

It is also advisable for the vocational rehabilitation expert to communicate with the forensic economist to determine who will be addressing the issue of worklife expectancy. The vocational rehabilitation expert using the RAPEL methodology may prefer to rely on one specific treatise that addresses worklife expectancy. If the forensic economist in his report prefers another treatise upon which to base worklife expectancy, this conflict could have a significant impact on the economic calculations. Therefore, it is better that all experts communicate in areas where methodology can create an overlap in areas of opinion.

6.13 Summary

The vocational rehabilitation expert is the only expert who can reliably set forth the pre- and post-injury earning capacity of an individual, unless the individual has worked for a long enough period of time pre-injury for another expert, such as the forensic economist, to conclude that continued employment in that job was probable. The vocational rehabilitation expert is the only individual with the background, training, and expertise to understand the impact of residual functional capacity, functional limitations, and a medical condition on one's ability to work post-injury. The vocational rehabilitation expert must rely upon records provided to her as foundation for her opinions. Paramount in this foundation are medical records and opinions of medical experts. I will not discuss the controversy regarding functional capacity evaluations as the means of providing information regarding the plaintiff's residual functional capacity except to say that in this author's opinion, based on the research, many functional capacity evaluations are simply unreliable in providing useful data by the vocational rehabilitation experts. While there are some functional capacity evaluation methodologies that have been subjected to peer review and are discussed in the literature, the majority are not. Those who administer functional capacity evaluations may also be poorly qualified to administer them. These factors, combined with the tendency to be over-reliant on subjective complaints without an objective basis for them, indicate to me that the most reliable source of providing information on post-injury functional outcome is a medical doctor. Certainly, the courts have recognized the credentials of a physician as being paramount in this area and usually require that there be medical foundation to support any vocational rehabilitation opinion.

Choosing a vocational rehabilitation expert should be done with caution, as choosing the wrong expert can have disastrous results to the case. Similarly, expecting other experts to perform tasks best left to the vocational rehabilitation expert is also a recipe for disaster. What I refer to here is the historical reliance on forensic economists to offer opinions regarding pre- and post-injury earning capacity when most forensic economists are not vocational rehabilitation experts and are simply incapable of doing so.

The astute attorney will recognize that each expert has a specific role in the case to measure lost wages and lost earning capacity. Choosing experts who are respected by attorneys who represent both plaintiffs and defendants should also be done wherever possible. An expert who can demonstrate a balanced retention by attorneys representing both plaintiffs and defendants is an expert with credibility. This expert has built such credibility by being consistent in his approach regardless of what side has historically retained him. The vocational rehabilitation expert who is retained exclusively or more often by one side or another is the expert to be avoided.

Chapter 7

Issues of Life Care Planners and Medical Care Costs

Ann T. Neulicht, Ph.D., C.L.C.P., C.R.C., C.V.E., C.D.M.S., L.P.C., D-ABVE and Frank Slesnick, Ph.D.

7.1 Introduction

The purpose of this chapter is to provide an introduction to life care planning and discuss the relationship between a life care planner and an economist. The chapter will cover the following topics: (1) What is a life care plan? (2) What is the education/training required for a life care planner? (3) What is the role of the life care planner within the legal setting? (4) How is a life care plan developed? (5) How should the life care planner communicate effectively with other experts, including the economist? (6) What are some special issues that arise when calculating the economic cost of a life care plan?

7.2 What is a Life Care Plan?

The term life care plan first appeared in *Damages in Tort Actions* (Deutsch and Raffa, 1981). A life care plan is a "dynamic document based upon published standards of practice, comprehensive assessment, data analysis and research, which provides an organized, concise plan for current and future needs with associated costs, for individuals who have experienced catastrophic injury or have chronic health care needs" (International Academy of Life Care Planners, 2006). The plan provides an individualized set of recommendations designed to assist a client in achieving optimal outcomes and preventing complications (Deutsch and Sawyer, 1985, Rev. 2005). When possible, the plan should be a collaborative effort among the treatment team members to reflect goals that are preventive and rehabilitative in nature as well as to provide accurate and timely cost information. It may provide health education, include recommendations for evaluations or treatment that contribute to the client's level of wellness, as well as provide information regarding treatment options that can be used by a client and other interested parties (e.g., Deutsch and Allison, 2004; Weed and Berens, 2000; Riddick-Grisham, 2003; 2006).

The goals of a life care plan are to facilitate an environment whereby an individual can become independent and participate in society to the greatest extent possible while living in the least restrictive environment. An individual's ability to work, need for recreation, and other personal growth activities are considered. In taking this whole person approach, the major premise is to restore an individual as close to the pre-incident lifestyle as possible. Entries must be based on a solid medical and rehabilitation foundation.

Life care planning has been applied to cases involving children and adults who have experienced catastrophic injuries such as brain injury, spinal cord injury, cerebral palsy, and chronic illness such as HIV, Hepatitis C, and renal failure (e.g., Riddick-Grisham, 2004; Weed, 2004). Aging with a disability has emerged as a significant planning issue as has pain management. Non-judicial uses have also been made of the technique of life care planning (e.g., discharge/educational planning, management of health care resources, geriatric care, health insurance referrals, rehabilitation facilities/programs).

7.3 Education/Training of a Life Care Planner

Life care planning practitioners may include, but are not limited to, individuals with primary occupations such as nursing, rehabilitation counseling, medicine, physical/occupational/speech therapy, or psychology. Life care planners must possess the appropriate educational requirements as defined by their professional standards and typically maintain licensure or national board certification within a health care discipline while engaging in life care planning activities. A professional discipline must provide sufficient education and training to assure that the life care planner has an appropriate medical foundation and an understanding of the health care delivery system and standards of practice/clinical practice guidelines. While assessment, research, analysis of data, and care recommendations are key functions of life care planning, the life care planner does not assume decision-making responsibility beyond the scope of practice for that profession as determined by state or national bodies. Practitioners are also responsible for following the standards of practice for life care planning.

As with any expert, a life care planner must be able to critically analyze data and demonstrate excellent written/verbal communication skills. A competent life care planner must not only have professional qualifications, but also must have completed coursework specific to life care planning, have a current awareness of trends in the field as well as a commitment to the profession. Standards of performance also include ethical issues and participation in research.

A variety of training programs in life care planning have evolved to provide detailed instruction on the format, methods, and procedures involved in outlining future care needs and costs in catastrophic cases. Training programs are now offered through several universities, as an online program (Kaplan College, University of Florida), home study program (A-PLUS-CES) and through organizations such as KELYNCO. Books and publications provide information about life care planning and address disability-specific as well as practice issues including procedures, services, technology, ethics, and standards (e.g., Weed, Berens and Deutsch, 2002).

In addition to education/training, a life care planner may take formal steps to show specific knowledge and expertise in life care planning through certification. The CDEC (now Commission on Healthcare Certification, or the CHCC) administered the first Certified Life Care Planner (CLCP) examination in 1996. There are now over 865 Certified Life Care Planners. A qualified health professional with an entry-level academic degree must complete an approved training program, submit a plan or complete a practicum/internship experience, and pass an examination for certification. Forty-eight hours of approved continuing education are required every three years for renewal.

The first Certified Nurse Life Care Planner (CNLCP) credential was awarded in 1998 and there are now more than 350 nurses who have obtained this certification. Certification through the American Association of Nurse Life Care Planners Certification Board is restricted to registered nurses with case management experience as well as contact hours from an approved training program or specific life care planning experience. Sixty points of credit are needed every five years for renewal of the CNLCP.

Fellow status is a distinction awarded by the International Academy of Life Care Planners (IALCP). Ten criteria are utilized to evaluate candidates and include health care license or certification, professional activities, continuing education, completion of at least fifty plans, and sworn testimony. The CHCC has just initiated a Fellow designation for individuals who have a minimum of a bachelor's degree, and certification as a CLCP, in good standing, for five years. The process requires successful completion of a written and oral examination.

7.4 Roles of the Life Care Planner

A life care planner can help an attorney develop case information, find experts, research issues, prepare deposition questions, evaluate the work of other life care plan or rehabilitation experts, provide a medical cost projection, and/or prepare a life care plan. A life care planner may be retained as a consultant to the attorney or as a testifying expert. In that case, the consultant provides "behind the scenes" information and is not retained to provide expert testimony. If retained as an expert in a litigated case, work completed is discoverable and the expert's name must be revealed/listed with the court.

A review of a life care plan, while professional and objective, critically looks at the methodology of the life care planner. A planner's background, training, and experience may also be addressed. The Checklist for Review of a Life Care Plan and/or utilization of a grid that compares the step-by-step procedures for developing a life care plan can also be used as a framework to provide comments on record review, adherence to published standards/procedures, and appropriateness of entries (Weed, 2004). PEERS Review (Neulicht, 2006) outlines issues to consider in the analysis of a plan and is included in the CD for this chapter.

The functions and skills of life care planning include assessment, data collection, planning, collaboration, plan development research, facilitation, evaluation, consultation, and testimony. The "glue" that holds a plan together, however, is the rehabilitation professional who serves the role of a general contractor with specific life care planning training and experience (Weed, 2002). A life care planner provides recommendations within his area of expertise (e.g., vocational, case management, counseling, ADL assessment), uses clinical knowledge to request specific information from treatment providers, and pulls all the information together into an internally consistent product.

The life care plan provides a foundation to assist an attorney in distinguishing pain and suffering, loss of enjoyment of life, and other non-economic aspects of the claim. It may assist in identifying other professionals, and may serve as a checklist and template for other testimony at trial. Properly prepared, a complete life care plan highlights the individual nature of the injuries and presents the specifics of the person's needs to all decision makers. Therefore, a life care planner must be able to clearly describe the purpose of each item of treatment and care described in the plan. In other words, "what it is, how it works, where and by whom it is performed, why it is needed, how it will help and what will happen if it is not provided" (Frick, 2003, p. 166).

7.5 The Life Care Planning Process

The job of a life care planner is to "view a situation, determine needs/variables, and formulate a plan to meet the individual's needs" (McCollom, 2004, p. 130). Life care plan methods include use of published checklists and forms, clinical practice guidelines, consultation with treatment team members (e.g., physicians as well as other healthcare professionals) to obtain individualized recommendations, and confirmation of projections with treatment team members and the client. Costs must be relevant and representative of the geographic area or region. Further the life care plan must take into account the actual cost to maintain the services required and not just the prevailing rate for such costs.

The step-by step procedure for life care planning typically begins with case intake and a comprehensive medical records analysis. This is followed by review of supporting documentation, initial interview arrangements and materials, consultation with team members, preparation of preliminary opinions, research of sources/costs, finalization of the plan and distribution of it to all appropriate parties. These items will be explained below.

As summarized by Riddick-Grisham and Taylor (2006), upon referral, the life care planner will typically request all medical/hospitalization, rehabilitation, physician, and home health records (including pre-incident records as appropriate to identify pre-existing conditions which could impact future medical or psychosocial needs and/or medical needs that are outside the scope of a life care plan). In pediatric cases, the life care planner will also want to review school records. Medical bills are frequently requested so as to track usual and customary care. Bills can also provide historical documentation of the frequency of disability-related complications and costs for both routine care and acute intervention such as emergency room visits. When obtaining hospital bills, it is helpful to request a document called the UB-92, as this provides medical coding information to a life care planner. Diaries and videotapes compiled by the client and family can provide the life care planner with valuable insights into the day-to-day demands of caring for an individual who has been injured. Review of the various depositions of treatment providers, employers, family members, and others is also necessary so that the foundation for a life care planner's recommendations is complete.

A crucial step in the development of a life care plan is the interview with the individual and family. When possible, this interview should be conducted in the setting where the individual resides, with corollary visits to therapy sessions, school, or work. An interview allows the life care planner to assess an individual's or family's knowledge of disability and coping strategies. It may provide information on discrepancies in treatment or new developments not yet reflected in the medical records. The life care planner can also examine medical equipment and develop a comprehensive list of medications and supplies. Information regarding accessibility and safety as well as observation of family dynamics can be obtained from these visits. When necessary, interviews with family members, separate from the client, may allow for candid discussion of limitations and concerns.

The next step in the completion of a life care plan involves collaboration with the treatment team. Although medical records may include future recommendations for treatment as well as historical information that support the need for additional evaluation and treatment, it is rare that treatment providers include lifelong recommendations in their notes. The team may involve several physicians or extend to therapy, school, or other community providers including home health agencies and staff. Soliciting input from team members based upon their involvement with a client is necessary to provide a foundation for plan entries. It is not uncommon for the life care planner to identify areas that require additional exploration or evaluation. The process of "filling in the holes" can include telephone or personal consultation with treatment team members to provide answers to specific questions regarding prognosis, long-term needs, and referral for further evaluation.

Each life care plan is specific to an individual and injury; however, areas typically considered include:

- projected evaluations
- routine medical care
- diagnostic testing
- surgical intervention
- aggressive treatment
- medications
- projected therapeutic modalities
- wheelchair needs
- wheelchair accessories and maintenance
- aids for independent function
- orthotics/prosthetics
- durable medical equipment
- supplies
- transportation
- health and strength maintenance
- home care
- facility care
- architectural renovations

Based on past history, input from team members, relevant literature, and clinical practice guidelines, the life care planner determines the items and services needed in each category, along with their beginning and ending dates, frequency of replacement, duration, and associated costs. Only items that are probable (more likely than not) for an individual are included in a plan. Although potential complications or future technology may be issues for an individual, costs cannot be accurately predicted. It is generally accepted that the life care planner will research costs in the geographic locations where the individual and family reside. Use of an existing vendor or agencies that are recommended by the treatment team provides a usable "roadmap" for the family. Obtaining several quotes allows the life care planner to demonstrate average costs or a cost range. Local vendors as well as online resources may be included for entries such as durable medical equipment and medications (especially if an individual already orders via web-based companies). Further, use of multiple sources of data enhances opinion validity (Barros-Bailey and Neulicht, 2005).

7.6 Communication With Case Experts and Other Professionals

Life care planning is a complex endeavor that requires multiple steps to complete. Often review of the medical records and client/family interviews can be completed relatively quickly. If additional evaluations are needed, adequate time must be allowed to complete the evaluation, obtain results, and research the cost of recommendations. Therefore, communication with a variety of experts and other professionals is critical.

A. The vocational expert

In cases where a vocational expert is providing an opinion on loss of earning capacity and another expert is researching and preparing a life care plan, it is imperative that both communicate with each other and provide opinions that are consistent. If the life care planner opines that an individual requires twenty-four-hour care and the vocational expert establishes that the individual can return to work without the need for a full-time aide, this discrepant information could call into serious question the validity of both reports.

B. School and treatment professionals

The life care planner must be aware of the impact of recommendations in a plan. Typically a fifty-two-week therapy year is not utilized as both families and therapists take time for vacations and holidays. For children, therapies provided in the school setting must be considered in addition to that which is medically relevant (not solely for educational function). Also, it may not be realistic for a child to go to school, then participate in speech therapy three times per week, occupational and physical therapy three times per week, go to a horseback riding lesson, and have multiple doctors' appointments as well. This may require coordination of visits and/or assistance for the family (e.g., home health assistance to transport the child or babysitters for other children in the family). Consideration of developmental milestones is necessary. For example, parents of "normal" infants assume that they will have twenty-four-hour responsibilities for feeding, diapering, and supervising. It is not typical for these parents to have the same level of responsibility for a nine-year old that wears diapers and is tube fed. Thus, plan entries must take into account these disability-related needs. Recommendations for attendant care must also be reduced during periods of school, specialized camp, or work unless an individual aide or job coach is also required at these times.

C. The physician

If multiple doctors and other treatment providers are involved, the life care planner must ensure that recommendations are consistent. In some cases, this may require resolution of conflicting opinions. In instances where physician opinions are similar but differ in frequency only, then a range may be provided. For example, two physicians recommend the same blood work, but at different frequencies due to a difference in the medications prescribed; both sets of recommendations may be appropriate and expressed as a range of frequency and cost.

D. The economist

Once the life care plan has been developed, it is necessary for the economist to estimate the present value of the plan. How do the life care planner and the economist ensure that there is good communication between these two experts?

Whenever a life care plan (LCP) is developed, it is almost always necessary to hire an economist to estimate its cost. There are a number of issues that need to be addressed so that both experts are on the same page. Perhaps the most important is that the LCP be presented in a format so the economist can easily understand what costs should be considered. Costs should be broken down by category since many forensic economists analyze an LCP according to individual components of the Medical Care Price Index (MCPI). For example, it is helpful if the life care planner distinguishes prescription and non-prescription drugs and hospital and non-hospital services. For each category, the economist needs to know the base cost, how often the item will be needed per year, and for how many years. The LCP should also reduce uncertainty as much as possible. It is reasonable to provide a range for initial costs and even indicate that certain items may or may not occur in the future. But it is important that the LCP make clear how the economist should consider uncertainty. For example, if a surgery may occur in five years at a cost of $20,000, this entry can be included in the life care plan without a date or as a footnote (and thus not included in estimating a total cost). It should be noted that if the LCP is not clear, it is always possible for the economist to simply call the life care planner to clarify its meaning. Such interaction is common, and should be encouraged to avoid future misunderstanding.

A second issue is that all medical costs in a life care plan should arise from the injury being considered in the lawsuit. Routine medical services that most individuals incur would not be included. If a special van is needed, normally it is necessary to deduct the cost of a car that would be purchased without the special added equipment.

A related issue concerns attendant care and household service, which is frequently the most expensive part of a life care plan. Due to physical or cognitive limitations, an injured party may require help with ADLs (Activities of Daily Living), which can include routine household services such as general cooking, cleaning, shopping, and housecleaning. If the plaintiff is also claiming lost household services, then it is important to distinguish such services specifically related to the injury and services that are claimed elsewhere in the lawsuit. Admittedly, it is often difficult to make this type of separation both for household services and other areas such as medical services, the cost of an automobile, and renovating a home.

7.7 Specific Economic Issues Related to Life Care Plans

The following are a few issues that the economist must consider when calculating the cost of a life care plan.

A. Accepted medical costs

Future medical costs should meet three criteria. (a) They must be directly related to the tort. (b) They are generally accepted by the medical profession. (c) They are reasonable in amount. The first was examined above when discussing the concept of incremental costs. The second is based on recommendations from treatment or consulting physicians, typically obtained through specific questions posed by the life care planner. Only items and services that are medically necessary are included in a plan. The third is a multi-dimensional issue. One dimension refers to the cost of each specific item. Based on research and contact with vendors, the life care planner provides private pay quotes that are reasonable and customary in the relevant geographic area (obtainable by the client). Another issue that often arises is differing plans provided by life care planners for the same individual. As an example, an individual who has suffered a spinal cord injury will often need an attendant. Should the attendant be an RN with special training or an individual with lesser training? How many shifts are required to assist the individual? Medical recommendations must be considered, as well as the type of care and functions of a caregiver (e.g., Is skilled care necessary? Is an attendant who remains "awake" at night necessary? Is home care versus facility care needed?) Variations typically result from differences in clinical knowledge and judgment among life care planners, experience in the life care planning process, as well as failure to consider Standards of Practice in plan development (McCollom, 2004).

B. Life expectancy

Perhaps the greatest source of uncertainty when there is a catastrophic injury is the life expectancy of the individual. There is significant literature that indicates that, for certain injuries, a reduced life expectancy should be examined (Slesnick and Thornton, 1999; Lewis, 1995; Ciecka and Goldman, 1995). Unlike the estimate of lost earnings, medical costs will be reduced proportionately if life expectancy is reduced since the life care plan is obviously designed to provide funds for the period the person is alive. However, even if it is decided that a reduced life expectancy should be introduced into evidence, there is still the question of who will make that determination. A physician could make that estimate, but physicians often are not familiar with the methodology utilized in estimating life expectancy. An alternative is to hire an expert who is familiar with large databases of similarly situated individuals (Strauss et al., 2001). It should be noted that the problem of estimating life expectancy could be circumvented with the purchase of a life annuity. (See Chapter 14 for details and cautions.) The individual's medical records are submitted to an insurance company that will offer a price for an annuity that will pay for medical costs. A life annuity will continue paying as long as the individual is still alive so there is no need to make such an estimate beforehand. As a final point on this topic, life expectancy may be an issue with regard to the plaintiff's current condition, the usual case, but also her condition prior to the tort. For example, an individual who was in a serious automobile accident may have been a heavy smoker prior to the accident.

C. Net discount rate

As explained in Chapter 3, it is important to estimate both the rate of increase in earnings and the interest rate that discounts future losses back to the present. The difference between these two values is called the net discount rate. Similarly, the economist will project future medical costs at some specific rate of increase and discount future costs back to the present. There is some controversy as to whether the forecast for the rate of increase in medical costs should be broken down into separate components such as hospital costs, attendant costs, prescription drugs, etc. (See Johnson and Gelles, 2000 for one view and Caragonne et al., 2000 for a contrary view.) What is generally accepted is that if only one index is utilized, it should not be the Medical Care Price Index (MCPI), which is heavily weighted toward hospital and physician costs—costs that usually are not major components of a life care plan. In terms of what rates will be forecast, medical costs have generally increased faster than all prices, although there was a brief period in the 1990s when that was not the case. The question is whether it is reasonable to forecast medical costs rising at a rate significantly faster than other costs over a long period of time, given that extending that differential into the future implies that the health care sector will grow larger and larger over time. Many forensic economists will provide a range of values for the net discount rate in life care cases.

D. Collateral source payments

The issue of collateral source payments enters the cost calculation when past or future medical costs are paid for by some outside source such as an insurance company or the government. As long as payments are received from an entity other than the defendant, such collateral source payments are usually not deducted from the loss estimate. There have been changes in some jurisdictions and for certain types of cases concerning what is or is not a collateral source. For example, some states require that certain education expenditures made for children with disabilities be considered as an offset. As Ireland and Pearson point out (2006), the life care planner will have to take account of these expenditures or make a case that public provision is not adequate, depending upon applicable law.

E. Tax issues

The issue of taxes with regard to medical costs is complicated. As discussed in Chapter 11, taxes will tend to lower future losses but also lower interest earned on the award so the impact on the present value of future loss could be higher or lower compared to ignoring taxes. However, with regard to medical costs, taxes will raise the award because the interest earned is lower but there is no comparable reduction in medical costs. If taxes must be considered, some forensic economists simplify the analysis by assuming investment in tax-free municipal bonds. However, the highest rated municipal bonds are still considered somewhat riskier than Treasury securities.

The CD for Chapter 7 contains three sections. The first section contains annotated economic references for citations in this text as well as some typical questions and answers posed to an economist in a deposition or trial setting. The second section provides life care plan references and additional life care planning resource information. The third section will continue the sample case analyzed in earlier chapters by providing examples of life care plan entries.

Chapter 8

Wrongful Death Cases and Personal Consumption Deductions

Michael L. Brookshire, Ph.D. and Elizabeth A.W. Gunderson, Ph.D.

8.1 Introduction

The *American Heritage Dictionary* defines consumption as "the using up of consumer goods and services" (p. 315). During a lifetime, a portion of your earnings goes towards paying for such things as food, clothing, and items that are particular to the way you spend time. In cases of wrongful death, the earnings are the basis for the loss, but the decedent is no longer able to make those purchases that went towards his sole enjoyment. As a result, consumption expenditures by a deceased must be deducted from lost earnings, because survivors would not have received any benefit from these dollars had the decedent lived.

The deduction for consumption is not as straightforward as one might think. In a household of two, for example, there are some costs that clearly benefit the decedent. But, there are also expenses that are jointly shared such as the mortgage or rent, heating, electricity or car insurance. With families that have children, more of the earnings will be devoted to the needs of the others in the family and to those joint expenses that still remain. The economist will review whatever information is available to make the appropriate determination for what the deduction for consumption should be.

8.2 The Differing Legal Parameters

The logic of a self-consumption deduction from estimated earning capacity, in order to make a survivor whole, seems clear. Yet, the self-consumption deduction is governed by at least three sets of legal parameters, which may result in widely different present values of the net loss of earning capacity to survivors. These three mandates to forensic economists are represented by six of the states in which one of the authors practices.

In Kentucky and West Virginia, no personal consumption deduction from earning capacity may be made by a forensic economist. A forensic economist may not testify about such a deduction, and even the concept of a personal consumption deduction cannot be mentioned by attorneys or economic experts on either side of the litigation. Since zero dollars are deducted, estimates of lost earning capacity are the highest in these two states versus the other four states being compared.

In Ohio and Virginia, expected or likely consumption is to be deducted from earning capacity. Whatever the method or data source used by an economist, all categories of spending by the deceased for her self-consumption are considered. The (net) loss of earning capacity is therefore much lower than in the no-deduction states, and this is especially true for younger persons and single persons.

Pennsylvania and Tennessee are "personal maintenance" deduction states. The self-consumption deduction is not what we expect that the deceased would have spent exclusively on himself. Rather, it is the spending he would have needed in order to maintain himself in such a condition of health and well being that he could have attained the earning capacity being estimated. The wording of the state Supreme Court decisions in both states is very similar, and, in both states, the income level of the deceased must somehow be considered. Moreover, the nature of the maintenance deduction differs in one respect, even between these two states. In Pennsylvania, the economist is to include a deduction for "some recreation," whereas this is not a part of the deduction in Tennessee. Obviously, the (net) loss of earning capacity is higher than in expected consumption states.

8.3 Alternative Methods and Data Sources

For those states that require a deduction for consumption, the economist may consult with the family of the deceased to determine what the spending patterns were. The economist will be interested in learning whether the deceased was typical in her spending habits, or if she exhibited some unusual patterns that might be the result of a hobby, a medical need or some other difference, or alternatively, frugality. This information will not be used to specifically calculate the consumption deduction, because it is based upon the records and memory of the family members, and as such is not very reliable. The economist is looking for patterns that are not typical or that are significantly different from what would be described as the average amount spent on personal items, but, in practice, specific investigation of spending patterns is not common, and use of statistical data on consumption is the rule.

One approach used by economists to determine the appropriate percentage for consumption is to utilize the research results of specific journal articles or to combine the percentages from several studies. The literature is rich with studies that estimate a consumption percentage based upon income level, family size and gender. The CD accompanying this book lists these articles and provides electronic links to them.

Once the consumption percentage is selected, the loss calculation is straight-forward. Estimated earning capacity for each year is reduced by the estimated self-consumption of the deceased, had he lived. Assume that the estimated salary earnings for a deceased worker were $40,000 for a particular year. If the personal consumption deduction is estimated as 30 percent of earnings, for example, this is $12,000 in the particular year. The net loss of earning capacity in salary earnings is therefore $28,000 ($40,000 minus $12,000) to a surviving spouse with no children in the home. A Jackie Travis sample case is adapted to a consumption example in the CD section for this chapter.

A second approach used by forensic economists is to calculate the self-consumption percentages out of earnings by using data from the Consumer Expenditure Survey (now labeled CEX) data of the U.S. Department of Commerce. This data source allows the consumption percentage to be differentiated by income level of the household and shows data by spending category. These "benchmark" data are used for specific plaintiffs primarily because necessary records do not exist for a reliable estimate of spending by the particular person. Moreover, the same source data may be used in personal maintenance states as well as actual (expected) consumption states. As children reach majority age, or if other changes occur in household size, percentage adjustments taken from the CEX data should change accordingly.

Personal maintenance expenditures are logically less than expected actual consumption (total expenditures). Whatever categories of spending are included in the Consumer Expenditure Survey data for expected consumption of a deceased person, a maintenance deduction must mean fewer categories of spending and/or less-than-100-percent spending as indicated for some categories. Some examples of spending categories that would not seem to represent "maintenance" consumption are alcoholic beverages, entertainment, reading, and tobacco products. It will be recalled that one of the maintenance deduction states provided that "some recreation" expenditures be included in the personal maintenance deduction, while the other state did not. In the case of "some recreation," 50 percent of the expected consumption from the government categories of "above-maintenance" spending might be added to the maintenance deduction. Finally, it should be noted that some forensic economists estimate a maintenance deduction by using poverty level spending estimates.

The accompanying CD provides Consumer Expenditure Survey tables and raw data, which allow comparisons of the expected consumption, or maintenance, deduction from income. These percentage deductions vary by gender, income range, and household size. For example, the death of a $60,000 earner in a three-person household means a 24.5 percent reduction from earning capacity for expected, actual consumption by a male (25.1 percent female); an 11.9 percent (12.5 percent) personal maintenance deduction; and a 13.6 percent (14.2 percent) deduction if "some recreation" is added to maintenance spending. The percentage deductions for single persons are much higher, as expected.

One complication is accounting for self-consumption out of retirement earnings. Economists use two approaches. The first takes consumption out as the retirement investment is made. In our example of a $40,000 annual salary earner, assume that 7.5 percent of this salary would have been paid into a tax-deferred retirement account for the earner who is now deceased by the employer. If 30 percent of these pension values, when received, would have been spent for self-consumption by this person, the 7.5 percent of $40,000 value can be reduced by 30 percent to 5.25 percent of $40,000 as loss to a spouse survivor. A $3,000 annual loss value at 7.5 percent becomes a $2,100 net loss of earning capacity in employer-provided fringe benefits. Under this approach, the analysis for lost earnings would stop at the end of the deceased's worklife expectancy because his consumption during retirement is already in the analysis. An alternative approach would be to invest the retirement funds until the worker were to retire and then deduct the consumption amount using an appropriate percentage as the funds would likely be used during his retirement years.

8.4 Two Earner Households

Up to this point, we have sidestepped the issue of whether the decedent was the sole breadwinner for the family or whether the decedent is in a two-earner household. The question becomes whether consumption should be taken from either the earnings of the family (including the earnings of both spouses) or whether the earnings of the decedent alone should be considered for consumption. An example is in order.

Assume that our $40,000 female worker Mrs. Doe was married to Mr. Doe, who was the same age and also earning $40,000 annually. When Mrs. Doe was killed, what was the net loss of earning capacity to her surviving husband? Considering Mrs. Doe's earnings alone, the personal consumption deduction at a 30 percent rate would be $12,000, and the net loss of earning capacity would be $28,000 in that particular year.

The loss estimate changes dramatically if the 30 percent self-deduction for consumption by the deceased is applied to total family earnings of $80,000 per year. The consumption deduction from the earnings of the now-deceased worker becomes $24,000 ($80,000 x 30 percent) per year, and the net loss of earning capacity is only $16,000 per year ($40,000 – $24,000). Depending upon the relative amounts of earnings by the two adult earners, there could be no net loss of earning capacity to the surviving adult. On the other hand, the application of a deceased-income-only theory of net loss to a deceased with much lower earnings than the surviving spouse produces a silly result as described below.

Again, the CD provides calculations for the Jackie Travis case carried throughout the book. The CD also provides substantial information on how the assumed 30 percent actually varies by income level and family size, and it shows survey results on current practices of forensic economists. According to the most recent survey of forensic economists, slightly over half of the respondents used only the decedent's earnings to calculate a consumption deduction rather than the total family income; slightly under half deducted from total family income. Clearly this issue remains unresolved by practicing forensic economists, and the impact upon loss estimates in specific cases can be very large.

Some of the reasoning that has been given for both alternatives follows:

Consumption Percentage Applied to Decedent's Income

- The decedent's consumption amount from the spouse's earnings represents a gift on the part of the spouse and should be considered a collateral source.
- The maxims of equity require that the defendant should not benefit from her wrongdoing. The surviving spouse should not have his economic loss reduced or completely eliminated because the surviving spouse happened to work and earn income.
- The surviving spouse would not be *forced* to work, as under the total family income method, in order to be made whole.
- Taking consumption out of deceased's income may partially or completely offset the fact that the economist is not calculating less tangible categories of damages, such as the enjoyment of life, and such damages are increasingly capped.

Consumption Percentage Applied to Total Family Income

- Every study by economists on consumption percentages out of income provides consumption percentages by one person out of total family income. Thus, applying these percentages to only the deceased's income is unscientific and incorrect.

- Forensic economists cannot invent applications of the collateral source rule or use their inability to calculate other categories of damages as justification for the unscientific handling of a consumption deduction in a two-earner family.
- It is true that in specific cases, no net loss of earning capacity exists to a much-higher-income survivor. However, it is the deceased-income-only method that produces nonsensical results when extreme examples are used. If spouse A earned $10,000 per year and spouse B earned $1 million per year, would the deceased A have been spending 30 percent of $10,000 per year or 30 percent of $1,010,000? Both academic studies and common sense suggest the answer is 30 percent of the $1,010,000 in total family income.

The State of California requires that only the earnings of the decedent should be considered in the analysis. It is clearly important for the attorney and the economist to determine the applicable laws for their venue, and both the plaintiff and defense attorney need to know the past position of their economist on this issue; it better be consistent!

8.5 Single Persons

A case resulting from the death of a single person is either brought on behalf of the estate of the decedent or on behalf of survivors who are typically parents and sometimes siblings. The approach taken by the economist may depend upon which of these is true.

When the suit is brought on behalf of the estate, the analysis is much the same as what has been presented here. The personal consumption percentage increases dramatically because those items that were previously considered to be jointly shared are no longer shared with anyone. For example, heating costs that were a benefit to both people living in the home now only benefit the decedent and are included in personal consumption. Where the consumption percentage had been 30.5 percent for a married female, it is between 65.8 percent and 74.8 percent for a single female at the same earnings level (Ruble et al.). The percentage of consumption for single persons has also averaged 80 percent of earnings in survey studies of forensic economists.

If a lawsuit is brought on behalf of the decedent's parents, for example, then the economist may focus the analysis on how the child was economically supporting the parents. In this case, consumption may not be part of the analysis, although the defense attorney may want to assure that the amount used to support the parents is reasonable in light of consumption. As always, legal parameters in the particular jurisdiction will guide economic loss calculations.

8.6 Final Comments

Unusual situations should be considered by the attorney and the economist in selecting a consumption percentage that falls under the "what if" category. What if there are physically or mentally disabled children at home? What if there are other adults, such as elderly persons, living with the family? Also, a relatively new issue is a self-consumption deduction from household services loss estimates, and this is discussed in Chapter 5, *Household Services Losses*.

The accompanying CD includes the analysis of a sample case and presents sources for personal consumption percentages with electronic links. Articles that are connected with the issue of consumption are also listed. The use of Consumer Expenditure Survey data in generating personal and maintenance consumption expenditures is shown in more detail. The consumption deduction percentages used in the (September 11, 2001-related) Victim's Compensation Fund formula are also shown. Finally, sample testimony segments are provided, which illustrate consumption deduction issues.

Chapter 9

Less Tangible Damages

Gerald Martin, M.B.A., Ph.D.

9.1 Background

Forensic economists have traditionally been permitted to measure certain types of damages and present their value to a jury. Other types of damages have traditionally been outside the range of damages to which an economist could testify. The first group is generally referred to as special damages, meaning damages to which specific dollar amounts can be attributed to either an injured or a deceased party. The latter group is typically referred to as general damages and has been left to the jury to determine without the assistance of an economist. Examples of special damages would be earnings, benefits, medical care costs, and the value of household services. General damages include items such as loss of companionship, loss of consortium, and the value of pain and suffering. In some states, general damages extend to the value of advice, counsel, and care. The value of these items is often taken from data available on the earnings of recreational workers, counseling workers, and religious counselors. This chapter will focus on just one of these general damages, originally called Hedonic Damages (HD) but in recent years more often referred to as the Value of the Pleasure of Life (VPL).

In 1985, economist Stan Smith opened a totally new frontier in calculating damages when he was permitted to provide dollar values to the jury on what he termed "Hedonic Damages" (*Sherrod v. Berry*, 629 F. Supp. 159 (N.D.Ill. 1985)). Hedonic Damages, in broad terms, is a measure of how an injured person or survivor of a deceased person would place a dollar value on the value of the pleasures of life. At first blush, this would seem to be a general damage, but the court allowed Smith to provide specific dollar amounts for the value of a statistical life. Since that testimony was allowed, there has been a continuing controversy among economists as to whether this is a valid calculation by an economist, whether it is based on statistical data that are relevant to such a calculation, whether the studies relied upon are really measuring what the economist says they measure, whether it is logical to attempt to compensate a dead person, whether there is any value short of infinity to compensate, say, a quadriplegic, whether the value of life is an overlap of any jury award for loss of companionship, consortium, and pain and suffering, and whether the quality of life of the individual prior to the incident should be used to adjust the value of the loss of the pleasure of life. On this latter point, assume two plaintiffs who, when injured, became quadriplegics. Suppose the first was in excellent health prior to her injury and the second was already a paraplegic who became a quadriplegic due to the incident. It can be argued that the plaintiff who was in excellent health had a higher value for the pleasures of life than did the paraplegic, who had already suffered a reduction in his quality of life prior to the current incident. These are certainly not easy questions for anyone to answer, including the economist.

Prior to the *Sherrod* opinion, there were no jurisdictions that specifically precluded the economist from making Hedonic Damage calculations and presenting them to a jury. Therefore, if we begin with the assumption that all jurisdictions were silent on whether the economist could make these calculations, we can now say that there are some jurisdictions that specifically preclude them and some that specifically permit them. For example, the State of Mississippi has prohibited the economist from presenting Hedonic Damage testimony by state law. Other states, such as California, now preclude them on the basis of appeal opinions (*Loth v. Truck-A-Way*, 60 Cal. App. 4th 757, 70 Cal. Rptr. 2d 571 (Cal. App. 1998)). On the Federal Court level, one opinion that eliminated the use of an economist to present these damages is *Ayers v. Robinson*, 887 F. Supp. 1049 (N.D. Ill. 1995). (Note that this is the same district from which the *Sherrod* opinion was published 10 years earlier.) In other jurisdictions where there is no specific opinion either allowing or disallowing such testimony, the battle is often fought by attorneys through motions in limine. New Mexico is an example of a state that specifically permits the economist to testify to the value of the pleasure of life (*Couch v. Astec Industries, Inc.*, 53 P.3d 398 (NM Ct. App. 2002)). Earlier opinions in New Mexico had left the issue up to the trial judge.

9.2 Survey of Economists

Economists who are active in the field of forensic economics also differ on whether VPL damages should be calculated and presented by the expert. Some argue that the existing willingness to pay and cost benefit studies provide the statistical framework for making such damage calculations. Others argue that these studies were not designed for such use and that the variability in results is so large as to make them meaningless. Over the last ten years or so, the National Association of Forensic Economists has sanctioned a series of surveys of members and one of the questions has to do with whether or not the members are willing to provide testimony on VPL.

In the 2003 survey, the question asked was:

> "A plaintiff's attorney asks you to calculate loss of enjoyment of life (Hedonic Damages) in an injury case. Would you be willing to calculate such damages?

There were 174 responses to this question with 17.82 percent saying they would be willing to calculate such damages. There were 82.18 percent saying they would not be willing to calculate such damages. A second question in the 2003 survey asks:

> "A defense attorney asks you to critique an economist's report that has calculated the lost enjoyment of life (Hedonic Damages) allegedly suffered by an injured plaintiff. Would you be willing to critique such a report?

Of the 174 respondents, 71.84 percent stated that they would be willing to critique such a report and 28.16 percent stated they would not be willing to make a critique. This survey implies that by a roughly three to one count economists would not calculate such damages and the same ratio would be willing to critique the report of an economist making the calculations.

These results must be tempered with a few qualifiers. Some states, such as California, have appeal opinions that preclude the introduction of Hedonic Damage testimony by economists. California has the largest number of practicing forensic economists of all the states, and it is possible that all California economists who answered the questionnaire said they do not offer such testimony simply because they may not, and not because they wouldn't be willing to do so. If this is also true in other jurisdictions that preclude Hedonic Damage testimony, then the number of respondents who reported they do not provide such testimony may be skewing the results of the survey. In essence, while the survey results indicate a quite large percentage reporting they will not provide such testimony, their responses may have been influenced by the judicial restrictions under which they operate rather than their personal preferences.

9.3 Measuring the Value of a Statistical Life

There are several methodologies employed in measuring the value of a life. For instance, one may measure the wage/risk differential. This measurement acknowledges that some occupations are inherently more dangerous than others, and that a higher wage should accompany the more risky jobs. Examples would be firefighters, military pilots, welders constructing high-rise buildings, and police officers who work in more crime prone areas. Cost/benefit studies are another method sometimes used. In these, the cost to implement, say, a safety measure in a factory that will reduce the number of deaths from five in 100,000 to two in 100,000 provides a means to arrive at a per worker saved value. In reality, the cost/benefit studies are just the larger studies with much of their data derived from the wage/risk differential. Stated differently, a cost/benefit study may be implemented where the costs relate to time and effort to install some safety device and the benefits may be based on the value of lives saved. The value of lives saved (benefits) can be measured by wages while the cost to save the lives can be measured by the price consumers are willing to assume to reduce the risk.

But the method that seems to have gained the lead in popularity is the willingness to pay method. In these studies, it is determined how much a person will be willing to spend to reduce her chances of death by some small probability. Probably the most often cited study is the smoke detector example. Suppose smoke detectors cost $25 and that they reduce the chance of death from two in 100,000 to one in 100,000, thus saving one life for every 100,000 smoke detectors installed. The total cost of 100,000 smoke detectors at $25 each gives a total expenditure by the group of $2.5 million. As this expenditure of $2.5 million results in the saving of one life, then the value of that life saved is assumed to be $2.5 million. This is a straightforward estimate that can easily be understood by a juror.

Critics, however, are likely to argue that the values can be distorted depending on whether the smoke detector was purchased cheaply at a discount store such as Wal-Mart®, or dearly at a specialty store such as Sharper Image®. They may further argue that one needs to know if the batteries used by the purchaser are the cheapest available or the highest quality available, or whether the owner actually replaces the batteries twice a year, as recommended. And, of course, they will argue that such a study is so general in nature that it applies only to a statistically average person and not to any specific plaintiff.

Dr. Ted Miller presented perhaps one of the most concise summaries of the studies in a paper ("The Plausible Range for the Value of Life: Red Herrings Among the Mackerel," *Journal of Forensic Economics,* Vol. III, no. 3, 1990). Miller examined sixty-seven studies and rejected twenty of them for containing flaws and methodological errors. In the remaining forty-seven studies, Miller made certain risk adjustments in an attempt to make all forty-seven comparable. The result is that he determined, from these forty-seven studies, that the value of a statistical life was $2.1 million in 1988 after-tax dollars, with a standard error of $650,000 and a range of $1.5 to $3 million. He then assumed thirty-six years remaining life expectancy and, after discounting to present value, estimated the annual value of Hedonic Damages (not Miller's term) to be $55,000 after-tax.

As would be expected, there are critics of the Miller results. One often-cited criticism is that while Miller's study may be well conceived, it was not done for the purpose of introducing Hedonic Damage estimates in court. Further, it deals only with a statistical person and not the specific plaintiff. Countering this argument, one can say that many other studies routinely relied upon by economists also were not designed for courtroom use and deal only with the statistical person. For instance, many economists use the Social Security Trustee's Report to estimate future wage changes and interest rates, but that report is created to illustrate the future funding for Social Security. Another criticism is that Miller made his risk adjustments in order to arrive at a rather "tight" distribution of results. The weakness of this argument is clear; there is no way to prove or disprove it. Given Miller's solid reputation as an economist, it seems unlikely he would have deliberately created the results.

Yet another question economists face is determining just what items are included in the Value of the Pleasure of Life. Suppose it is decided that the VPL for a particular plaintiff is $3 million. The question then arises as to whether the plaintiff's lifetime earnings and benefits are a part of the total amount. If they are, and assuming that those earnings are calculated to be $500,000, then should that amount be deducted from the VPL? It seems that most economists do assume lifetime earnings are part of VPL and an adjustment is made by deducting the earnings from VPL. The same arguments and conclusions can be applied to the value of household services.

9.4 Wrongful Death

The obvious question is whether or not it is possible to compensate a dead person for her value of life. The obvious answer is that it is not possible to compensate a dead person. However, the VPL of a spouse, child, sibling, or other close relative may be thought of as their loss of the companionship of the decedent. (The legal question is whether a VPL loss can be claimed by a person who is not a party (plaintiff) in the lawsuit.) This is certainly not easy for anyone, and the opponent of VPL testimony will argue that jurors should be allowed to make this determination without assistance from an economist.

Should the court allow economic testimony claiming a VPL loss by a surviving plaintiff, then the question arises as to whether the loss should be based on the VPL of the decedent or on the VPL of the plaintiff who has lost the pleasure formerly derived from sharing in the life of the decedent. In the late 1980s, the value to the decedent was the focus of the calculations and testimony. In more recent years, however, it seems to have shifted to valuing the loss to the survivors. Clearly, making such a calculation is difficult to do and difficult to explain ,and many questions abound. For instance, is the VPL of the decedent calculated using his life expectancy, earnings, household service value, etc., or is the emotional and physical loss suffered by the survivor to be calculated? Of course, it would be easier to focus only on the decedent, which leaves open the door for claims that the decedent cannot benefit from a VPL award. Focusing on the surviving plaintiff seems intuitively to be the logical approach, but there simply aren't any studies that examine the VPL of a surviving spouse or family member. It may be necessary to use a psychiatrist or psychologist to provide expert testimony regarding the impact of the death of the decedent on the surviving plaintiffs. It is obvious that this is not an easy task for any economist and leaves open many avenues of criticism from an opposing economist. The more interesting question here is whether these losses to survivors should even be classified as Hedonic Damages. It may be more appropriate to consider them as emotional damages, but several economists have continued to call them Hedonic Damages.

9.5 Personal Injury

In the personal injury case, there is no question as to whose VPL has been diminished. If we assume that it is possible to measure the VPL for a specific individual, then the prime mission is to somehow establish to what degree that VPL has been compromised. This now takes us beyond the expertise of the economist and requires additional testimony from either a mental health expert, a vocational rehabilitation expert, or both. Someone must testify to the quality of life enjoyed by the plaintiff prior to the injury and to the reduction in that quality resulting from the injury. Suppose the plaintiff was an avid skier, but has lost one or both legs. She certainly has lost the pleasure of enjoying something that formerly gave her a great degree of satisfaction. In other injury situations, there is always a question as to whether the loss of VPL is greater in the period immediately following the injury when the trauma effect is at its greatest, and whether the loss of VPL is diminished with time as the plaintiff learns to cope with his injury or disability. Or it could worsen with time as the plaintiff ages and deteriorates faster than would have been the case without the injury. The economist testifying to the VPL must of necessity rely on the input of mental health and vocational experts as to the percentage reduction the plaintiff has incurred, and whether this percentage increases or decreases over time.

Once the economist has this percentage reduction information, and assuming she is relying on the value for the statistically average person, then she need only adjust for the life expectancy remaining and the reduction in earning capacity and household service value to arrive at an estimate of the VPL loss. Typically the economist will not attempt to provide the jurors with a point estimate of the VPL loss, but will give them a range within which the jury can decide on the amount of the loss. It could be that the economist will estimate the VPL to be between, say, $500,000 and $1.5 million. While this may seem to be a large range, it is nonetheless at least a guideline for the jury.

9.6 Ancillary Material

Space limitation precludes adding sample reports in this chapter by an economist providing VPL testimony and the rebuttal of an economist on the other side. In the CD that accompanies this book, there is included a VPL report prepared by Dr. Stan Smith, probably the best-known advocate for making these presentations to a jury. Following that is a rebuttal report from Dr. Tom Ireland, arguably the best-known opponent of the calculation and presentation of VPL damages in court. You will note that the Stan Smith report and the Tom Ireland rebuttal are not for the same case. By using separate case reports and rebuttals, a larger scope of the controversy can be shown. In addition, there is an extensive number of readings available on this topic—far too many to include on the CD. Fortunately, there are texts and readings books available that have compiled all of the more significant research and writing, and these reference books are cited in the CD. It is also not necessary to include an exhaustive listing of appeal opinions as the most important are listed in the reference books.

Chapter 10

Some Special Cases and Issues

Michael L. Brookshire, Ph.D.

10.1 The (Lost) Earnings Base

Chapter 3 began the discussion of the selection of a wage earnings base, and there is no better example of how specific case circumstances may call for "special" treatment. Good forensic economics and common sense suggest that the (pre-injury) wage base—the annual wage earnings on which the future earnings will be based—should relate to the unique earnings history and/or skills of the particular individual. Generalized data should usually be used only when data on the specific person are unavailable. This is a damages estimate for that specific person rather than for a statistical class of persons. The base decision requires the most case-by-case judgment by a forensic economist. It is the first area of scrutiny and potential attack by the defense. Every calculation may be seen as an adjustment to the base, and errors in the base usually translate to proportionate errors in the lost earnings estimate.

Little research exists on the topic of selecting a wage base. As previously discussed, the decision is easy when annual earnings have steadily trended upward over many years. The base will be the last full year of earnings, adjusted by some wage growth factor to the first year of loss and then moved forward at some rate of wage growth. What if earnings steadily trended downward to the last full year before injury? Most, but not all, forensic economists would freeze this last full year as a loss base and argue against continuing a downward trend toward zero. They might grow this base by price inflation, which means holding it constant in "real" terms. These differences in method, and judgment, may substantially affect the loss estimate.

The earnings history may move up-and-down each year for such understandable reasons as cycles of a small business, overtime work, temporary unemployment, and so on. As suggested in Chapter 3, most economists will take an average of several years of past earnings to smooth out these cycles in estimating the future. Any average must be of dollars converted to the same year. If 2007 were the base loss year, all dollars in the average would first have been converted to 2007 dollars by increasing earlier values to 2007 values at the rate of price inflation. There is no agreement on the number of years to be averaged. It rarely exceeds five years, because longer periods are more relevant to decisions about the wage growth rate. Trial attorneys should tread carefully here and use their economist. In deciding among two to five years for the average, a guideline is to choose the number of years which best "captures" past ups and downs as they are likely to have been reflected in the "BUT FOR" future. An example focusing upon this issue ends this section.

In a specific case, the deceased or injured person may have one or more past years of very high earnings followed by several years of much lower, and steadily lower, earnings—a Wall Street broker has left the stress for a lower-paying career in his hometown. Most, but not all, forensic economists will ignore these high earnings years, unless a return to those annual years is somehow expected. Those who believe that earning capacity means the best ever attained or the highest earnings that could be obtained obviously choose a much higher base for their loss estimate. Indeed, there is significant debate about what the term "earning capacity" means as it may be measured in specific cases.

Special case facts may mean that an established earnings history should be ignored. Assume the wrongful death of a thirty-year-old custodian at a college of law, who has a ten-year history of full-time earnings as a custodian. Yet, this person had used the ten years and free tuition to obtain a bachelor's degree. Graduation as an MBA would have been three months after the incapacitating injury and the plaintiff had been actively interviewing for MBA jobs. The custodian wage history would not be used. Rather, an appropriate entry-level wage as an MBA might be selected.

Forensic economists disagree about whether or not, and how, earned income not reported on income tax returns should be considered. Special cases may vary from tips (likely) earned by a waiter to Schedule C income of a business proprietor, where costs have been maximized to lower taxable income. Some economists never vary from the stance that it is the income reported for taxes that must be considered in determining the lost wage base. Other economists may simply assume a percentage of reported wages in tips or recapitulate the Schedule C statements into a statement of cash flows for determining a base as a cash flow amount. Depending upon the size of depreciation expenditures especially, the second approach may result in a much higher lost earning capacity base. It is good to know if the damages expert being hired has an established position on this issue; the expert has a separate problem if she has not been consistent.

The first-year base for post-injury (residual) earning capacity is generally provided by a vocational/rehabilitation expert and is discussed in Chapter 6. The economist will rarely vary from this foundation but will typically ensure that actual, post-injury earnings don't differ inexplicably from the opinion of the vocational expert. The trial attorney should also realize that his expert might have automatically handled data issues that are not typically discussed. For example, partial-year earnings in the injury year may not be annualized and used in determining a wage base. Seasonality of earnings may make an annualized result unreliable and, more commonly, the partial year earnings on a W-2 may include one-time payments at injury or death for unused vacation and sick leave. Similarly, experienced economists will ensure that gross earnings are being considered, before IRA, 401(k), or other salary reduction amounts have been removed.

One sample case shows how difficult the earnings base decision may be and how experts may differ. Assume the case of a forty-year-old auto mechanic, whose ten-year earnings history before his December 31, 2006 death is as follows:

1997:	$32,050
1998:	$19,600
1999:	$22,314
2000:	$7,800
2001:	$33,000
2002:	$38,650
2003:	$8,460
2004:	$16,270
2005:	$31,045
2006:	$45,016

The judge has decided to allow evidence at trial that the periods of declining earnings are associated with documented drug and alcohol abuse, DUIs, treatment center and hospital stays, jail time, and significant periods off work. The plaintiff economist uses 2006 earnings for the earnings base, assuming that past problems have been corrected and the earning capacity of the last full year would have grown into the future. The defense economist uses the average of the last four years of earnings, assuming that this best represents the pattern of earnings over the entire historical period. He argues that the best assumption is that the pattern repeats in future years—he doesn't get better over any number of years, but he doesn't get worse. The earnings base estimate of the defense economist is almost 40 percent below that of the plaintiff economist. In fact, a forensic economist might make both estimates in the economic loss report and simply present the alternative estimates to the trier of fact. This may also be one of the exceptional circumstances where a vocational expert may opine on the *pre*-injury earnings base, and forensic psychologists and addiction experts may also become involved.

10.2 Some Special Issues of Age

Special estimation issues based upon age at injury or death are well represented by minor children at one extreme and retirement-age persons toward the other end of the age continuum. For persons injured or killed from birth to age eighteen, Chapter 3 already discussed the largest difference in earning capacity estimation—there is no (meaningful) earnings history to be used in estimating earnings flows but for the wrongful event. Most forensic economists assume one or more education levels and use a U.S. government data source that provides average wage or salary earnings by level of educational attainment, gender, race, and five-year age bracket. But how is the level of educational attainment chosen? The assumption should *not* simply come from the client attorney. The economist should have a logical and consistent method for making this decision, and the economist is likely to show two educational assumptions. This gives the jury a range and a sense of the loss difference with different educational attainments.

For a pre-school child, most forensic economists make their decision based upon the educational attainment of parents. If one was a high school graduate and one a college graduate, the economist may show results from both assumptions. An economist might also show one educational level above the highest attainment of parents, because children in the U.S., on average, have reached a higher educational level than their parents. Other predictors, such as the literacy status of the household, have been shown to be significant in the literature of forensic economics, and there is research toward attaching actual probabilities to different educational attainments based upon such variables. As the age at injury moves through the years of schooling, grades and standardized test scores increase in importance as common sense predictors of education level and earnings.

Since the government data source links education level to average earnings in five-year age categories, lost earning capacity estimates for minor children automatically include an age-earnings profile of earnings increases. A large literature in economics suggests a distinct earnings pay-off to investments in higher educational levels, and this is clearly shown in the escalating averages every five years until a leveling in the age forties and fifties. This increase is separate from assumed annual increases for price inflation and for productivity growth, although some overlap may exist with these other adjustments. The loss estimate increases significantly when a profile is used, so that defense attorneys also need to know good questions regarding the application of such profiles. The profiles may be used for some cases of college-educated adults, for example, but their earnings history should have followed earnings profiles at past ages, with inflation and productivity growth also considered.

Since earnings projections for minor children are made for many future decades, issues of appropriate wage growth rates versus discount rates mean a larger effect upon present value losses. Minor children are also a significant subset of single persons, and the personal consumption or maintenance deductions from earnings estimates, discussed in Chapter 8, are significantly larger than in other cases. Finally, costs of raising a child are estimated by the U.S. Department of Agriculture, and these costs and college costs may also be a deduction from economic loss as a matter of logic or state law.

Retirement-age persons might be defined as persons fifty-five or over at injury or death, and they present their own set of special issues. First, any age-earnings profiles from previous education will have "played out" and will not be a factor in projecting earning capacity. Secondly, labor force participation status (yes or no) at injury or death is especially important in estimating the future years of working life, and the worklife expectancy source data should allow for this differentiation. Third, a direct measurement of Social Security and defined benefit (private) pensions may show a very small pre- minus post-injury loss difference after retirement. Fourth, a forensic economist must increasingly deal with the possibility of phased retirement, a second career after a "primary" retirement, and reductions in average hours of work that are not captured under any of the methods for worklife expectancy. Fifth, there are common sense issues of how household service hours may decrease in old age. Finally, life care plan estimates of medical needs from doctor visits to diagnostic tests must be those beyond the needs of the general population, and these "normal" medical needs increase with age.

10.3 The Effects of Gender and Race

U.S. government data clearly show that both average earnings and the important, worklife expectancy variables—participation rates and employment rates—significantly differ by gender, race, and ethnicity. These differences are apparent in tables provided on the chapter CD. For adults with a work history, the earnings history for the particular person is used, and average earnings for statistical classes of persons are generally irrelevant to a forensic economist.

The same is not true for worklife expectancy, because the combination of participation and employment rates contained in any worklife expectancy measure has typically been based on statistical tables disaggregated by age, education level, gender, and race or ethnicity. For example, the participation rate for U.S. women (the probability that a female will either have a job or be in the workforce seeking a job) has steadily grown toward the rates of U.S. men since World War II, although their participation rate has leveled in recent years. It is still true, however, that the participation rate of women is just over 80 percent of the rate for men. The participation rates of black females exceed those of white and Hispanic females. Unemployment rates are lower for whites than for blacks or Hispanics. These differences do impact lost earning capacity estimates to the extent that forensic economists differentiate their worklife expectancy estimates by gender and race or ethnicity.

In a 2006 survey of members of the National Association of Forensic Economics (NAFE), those surveyed were asked if they used gender-specific data and race-specific data when such data were available and reliable. Of the respondents, 44.8 percent use both race-specific and gender-specific data, 0.6 percent use race-specific data only, 42.4 percent use gender-specific data only, and 12.2 percent do not use either race- or gender-specific data. This choice by a forensic economist may make a significant difference in the loss estimate for a particular case, and good questions may be asked to economists who either do or do not make these differentiations. For example, what if the participation rate gap of men over women closes completely over the next ten to twenty years? What if it widens? Should the uncertainty be resolved based upon the best, disaggregated data available or in favor of uni-sex participation rates? Beyond such issues of scientific prediction is the normative issue of whether forensic economists *should* differentiate estimates by gender and/or race or ethnicity. Many forensic economists believe it is their scientific duty to use reliable data that is as close as possible to the characteristics of the particular person. Others believe that discrimination is at least one factor in workforce differences by race and gender, and some believe that the use of data disaggregated by race and gender is morally or ethically wrong.

10.4 Special Occupations

For railroad, barge, and maritime workers, the legal parameters for calculating economic damages due to workplace injury are so different and special that a separate chapter of this book is dedicated to this set of occupations. Yet special issues exist, and may be anticipated, for many occupational groups. For example, the wrongful injury or death of professional athletes or entertainers may involve significant data gathering from industry sources as to likely changes in earnings as individuals age. Special features of compensation, such as residuals, may need to be explored. General worklife expectancy tables may not be very relevant, and after a "main" career, probable follow-up careers and earnings may need to be investigated—actors and actresses in supporting roles and sports broadcasters are examples.

Waiters, waitresses, small business persons and farmers have a common "special" feature affecting historical wage data used to estimate future lost earning capacity: their taxable earnings may be significantly less than their earning capacity each year. While changes in the tax laws have had some effect on the documentation of earning capacity in tips, income from tips remains underreported. Forensic economists differ on whether or not, or how, they will consider income upon which income tax was not paid. A farmer may have perfectly legal deductions that lower taxable income, and a small business person, especially if depreciation is a large factor in costs, will show lower profits than if cash flow analysis had been utilized. Again, a forensic economist, or accountant, who has practiced for may years, will likely have a history of his position on this special feature of otherwise unrelated occupations.

With executives, the forensic economist may obtain special salary survey data. She will face more complexity in the valuation of lost earning capacity in fringe benefits, especially as stock options are valued. Military and other uniformed occupations, such as police and firefighters, have special data sets but also share the characteristic that a primary career may last only twenty years, after which a pension is available and the probability of a second career is high. The assumptions about what happens in this occupational "switch" may obviously mean significant differences in lost earning capacity estimates.

Craft and other occupations may have more frequent than average periods of unemployment but may also have periods in which overtime earnings are significant. In one way or another, these variations by occupation that also would have occurred in the future must be "smoothed out." The possibility of more frequent occupational change and specialization in future years, and of outsourced jobs as another example, only increase the importance of necessary differentiations by occupation.

10.5 Special "Injuries"—Wrongful Termination

While this book focuses on economic damages in personal injury and wrongful death cases, wrongful termination cases are a good example of how damages issues may be different, and "special," when the nature of the "injury" differs. In cases of permanent physical or cognitive injuries, the pre-injury forecast usually extends through worklife expectancy. In wrongful termination, the pre-injury scenario ends, and therefore economic loss ends, when the individual would have left the employer defendant anyway, had the wrongful termination not occurred. Variables at issue include turnover rates, actual and likely layoffs after the termination, the tenure of the plaintiff with that employer, and the average length of employment by the plaintiff with past employers.

Another, major difference is that post-injury earning capacity may catchup with pre-injury earning capacity after some number of years. After all, there are no physical or cognitive injuries that permanently consign the plaintiff to lower paying jobs at lesser worklife expectancies. Special issues include the impact of any stigma from either termination or the pursuit of a wrongful termination lawsuit, U.S. government data on how fast displaced workers are re-employed and how long a wage gap below previous earnings remains, and how bad or good is the labor market for persons with the training and skill sets of the plaintiff.

A third major difference is that lost wages awards in wrongful termination cases are taxable to the plaintiff. The taxes on the lump sum in the year of an award will be higher than the sum of taxes on the wages that would have been received absent the wrongful termination. The literature in forensic economics addresses the necessary tax equalization, and the CD to this chapter links to published articles on all of these special issues in wrongful termination.

10.6 Summary and Conclusion

Basic principles, methods, data sources, and testimony issues concerning economic damages are described in this book. This chapter is a reminder that each case may have special features, cookie-cutter approaches to damages calculations may mean significant error, and both good judgment and a breadth of case experience are required of a forensic economist. Decisions on the earnings base are inherently special to the facts of a specific case; special issues arise by age, gender, race, and occupation; and special "injuries," such as wrongful termination, mean that data, method, and testimony will differ from personal injury cases. In the CD to this chapter, the reader may find detailed data on some of the differences that have been described, citations and links to other data, links to the relevant literature in forensic economics, and sample testimony Q&As demonstrating how some of the issues discussed above play out in testimony.

Chapter 11

The Special Issues of F.E.L.A. Cases

Jeffrey B. Opp

Synopsis

11.1 Calculating Damages under the F.E.L.A. for Injured Railroaders

Federal Employer's Liability Act (F.E.L.A.) cases are unique within the tort system. These cases involve employee versus employer personal injury actions, which outside of the F.E.L.A. would normally be the subject for a workers' compensation action. While damage calculations under most such cases would normally be a formulaic approach based upon statutes, under the F.E.L.A. such computations are left to the forensic economist to determine the appropriate method of calculation under the specific laws governing F.E.L.A. matters.

As has been noted in previous chapters, calculating losses for injured workers is not an exact science. However, the very nature of the railroads' seniority-based, unionized employment system provides tools and information that the forensic economist can utilize to provide accurate and individualized calculations. Most attorneys and forensic economists will understand that the use of detailed industry, craft, and individual information in the damage calculation presents a double-edged sword. As a result, some forensic economists take a more global approach to the calculation of damages. However, this chapter focuses on the detailed approach and addresses the wealth of information available in railroad cases, e.g., union contracts, earnings of individuals with similar seniority, and specific craft data, with which the forensic economist can be provided and consider when the information is available.

Legally-mandated differences in the actual calculations performed in injured railroader cases under the F.E.L.A. and other personal injury matters occur in two basic areas: 1) all calculations for lost wages are computed net of the federal and state income tax that the individual would have paid on the lost wages, and 2) rather than being subject to the Social Security Administration, craft railroaders fall under the Railroad Retirement Board, which has its own regulations governing employee and employer contributions and retirement ages. As can be expected, the calculation for income taxes varies significantly based upon the circumstances of the individual being evaluated. A single individual pays a higher percentage of his wages in taxes than a married individual with three children based upon the applicable tax rates, personal exemptions, and child tax credits. The Railroad Retirement Board also provides that an individual may, but is not required to, retire with an unreduced pension benefit when he reaches age sixty and has thirty years of service as a railroader. Individuals covered under the Social Security system must wait until at least age sixty-five for those born prior to 1937 and up to age sixty-seven for those born after 1960. Consequently, worklife expectancy may be affected by this difference.

Legal parameters aside, perhaps the most important issue in railroad cases is the fact that railroaders are subject to a seniority-based employment system. While this system is not specific to railroad cases, the forensic economist should be mindful of its effect on the wage loss calculation. The lost earnings base decision has been discussed in previous chapters, and many methods may be used: the last five years average, last two years average, a last year freeze, and others. An evaluation of what occurred in the past is used to project what would have happened in the future, barring injury. The seniority-based employment system renders most of these look-back methods moot. A railroader's earnings potential is not tied to what jobs he held in the past, but rather what jobs his seniority would have allowed him to hold in the future. An example of this concept can be drawn from the military, which is one of the most pronounced seniority-based employment systems. It would be inappropriate to calculate the future lost wages of a sergeant in the army based upon what he earned in the preceding five years when at a lower rank. The same is true for railroaders. It would be inappropriate to calculate the future lost wages of a foreman in the maintenance of way department based upon what he earned in the preceding five years when he was a track laborer. Future losses should be computed based upon the seniority at the time of injury going forward rather than looking back.

As was discussed in Chapter 10, understanding the case specific facts is important to an accurate damage calculation. In railroad cases, the importance of this understanding is compounded. Certainly the opposition attorney will be armed with these facts and it behooves the forensic economist to be similarly equipped.

11.2 Key Information

As discussed above, railroad cases place particular responsibility on the forensic economist to gather as much client-specific information as possible. Some of the areas of consideration are as follows. Beyond the normal dates utilized in personal injury cases such as date of birth, date of injury, last day worked, and others, railroad cases require an understanding of other key dates, such as the first date the railroader hired-out on the railroad. The seniority date for the railroader in his craft is often different. Both of these dates are important in understanding the individual's relative seniority and the number of railroad service months in the railroad industry. Family status of the railroader is also critical for a number of reasons. Income taxes that would have been paid on lost earnings and fringe benefits paid by the railroad vary based upon the marital status and dependents of the railroader. Consequently, the forensic economist should determine not only the railroader's marital status but also the ages of the dependents in order to accurately calculate income taxes and lost benefits. The craft of the individual, which normally includes engineers, conductors (trainmen) and maintenance of way workers, is also crucial. The craft is important not only for identifying the type of pre-injury work performed by the railroader, but also for identifying the railroader's union and the contracts applicable to the railroader.

11.3 Components of Railroader Earnings

Railroader compensation comes in many forms and is governed not only by current collective bargaining agreements, but also by protected class payments, special plans, and historical agreements. Understanding the craft of the injured railroader will generally give a road map of the types of compensation normally due. However, it is also important to evaluate the individual railroad's policies and procedures in order to accurately evaluate compensation. For instance, some conductors qualify for productivity payments based upon Crew Consist Agreements entered into between most major railroads and the United Transportation Union in the late 1980s and early 1990s. These agreements were put in place in order to compensate the union members for the removal of brakemen from operating locomotives and cabooses. Generally, conductors who were employed by the railroads at the time of the agreements receive a productivity share for each trip made. The value of this share is equal to a divided portion of the cost savings to the railroad for the lack of brakemen in a conductor's seniority district. In recent years, these productivity shares have become increasingly valuable as individuals retire and the cost savings is divided by fewer and fewer conductors within the seniority district. Alternately, some carriers have historically bought-out their conductors from their productivity shares and thus have no ongoing liability for such payments. Other examples of carrier-specific policies include the fact that several carriers have instituted an "attendance policy" which effectively limits the amount of time a railroader can lay-off before disciplinary action is taken. Consequently, the calculation for lost wages may be affected because a railroader will not be able to lay-off as much as he did on an historical basis. Further, due to the mergers that occurred in the railroad industry in the late 1980s and early 1990s, a number of railroaders are subject to "protected class" payments. This supplemental compensation is made in order to compensate railroaders for their loss of seniority and potential lower income that may have resulted from the merger. These are just two examples of the differences with the potential compensation of an injured railroader, but they highlight how crucial and important it is to understand the different policies and agreements governing railroader earnings.

The very nature of the seniority-based employment system leads to varying earnings from year to year. The typical age-earnings profile whereby a worker experiences higher than average increases in earnings in his first years of employment, a leveling-off during his middle years, and lower than average increases in his later years due to declining productivity generally do not apply to railroaders. For the most part, railroaders, when they first hire-out, will experience periods of lay-off during their first few years of employment. Their seniority is not sufficient to be able to hold a job full-time, as those with higher seniority will be able to out-bid them for these positions. Further, many carriers have a "new hire" policy whereby the newly hired railroader only receives 75 percent of his normal wage during his first year of employment with 5.00 percent annual increases until, after five years, he is receiving his normal wages. Both of these issues present a hurdle for the forensic economist in evaluating the projected future lost wages of an injured new-hire. This hurdle can be partially overcome by analyzing the historical wages of individuals with similar seniority to the injured railroader during the period between the date of injury and the present. This will allow the forensic economist the ability to make adjustments to the wages the injured railroader could have expected barring injury.

Once a railroader attains sufficient seniority to bid and hold full-time positions, his earnings are determined by the jobs he chooses to hold and work. As is true for all other workers, the railroader's job preference will be dictated by a myriad of factors, including family situation, financial situation, and health. Engineers with sufficient seniority can choose to work a road job wherein they run trains east and west from North Platte, Nebraska, for example. Alternately, they could choose to work a yard job wherein they operate trains in a local yard. Finally, they could choose to work a guaranteed extra-board which, provided they do not lay-off, pays them a set rate whether they are called to work or not. Generally, road jobs pay the most but are also the jobs that require the most time away from home. Yard jobs pay less, but the railroader is able to be at home. Guaranteed extra-board jobs are income-limiting but generally require the least time commitment. Seniority grants this freedom of choice for railroad workers.

Where railroad workers vary most profoundly from the age-earnings profile of the typical worker is in the latter years of employment. Typical workers will generally experience a slow-down in earnings increases in their last few years of employment. In contrast, because of the seniority-based employment system, railroad earnings can have the opposite result. Because railroader retirement benefits are weighted towards the last and highest years of earnings, many railroaders will choose to accelerate their earnings in these last few years. They are accommodated in this pursuit by the seniority-based system, which, due to their higher seniority in the final years of their work-life, allows them to hold the highest paying jobs. Often railroaders will describe these positions as the "gravy" jobs, which allow them to work at the same level, or perhaps even less, and yet garner higher wages.

11.4 Issues with Offsets to Railroader Earnings

Under the F.E.L.A., the calculation for lost earnings in railroad cases must be considered net of federal and state income taxes. Some forensic economists will choose to apply the income taxes as a single percentage rate to all future lost earnings while others will project the future dollar amount of the tax based upon current tax law and future earnings, exemptions, and deductions information. Regardless of the method used to calculate the tax, the inclusion of income tax in the calculation requires that the interest vehicle used to calculate the net discount rate be either tax-free, or expressed as its after-tax equivalent. This is crucial, as the present value of the loss represents a lump-sum that, when invested, will yield an amount, principal plus interest earnings, equal to the projected future loss amount net of income tax. Consequently, if the interest earnings on the lump sum are taxed, then the damage calculation has double-counted income taxes. While it seems intuitively obvious that the inclusion of income taxes in the calculation would result in a lower number, the use of the tax-free interest vehicle often negates the negative effect and, in some cases, causes a higher calculated amount.

In addition to federal and state income taxes, most state and federal courts hold that the calculation for lost earnings in railroad cases must be considered net of employee expenses and deductions the railroader would have been required to pay to obtain the lost earnings. Employee expenses can vary tremendously depending on the craft and job of the railroader. An example is a maintenance of way employee who works a line close to his home. Generally, his expenses would be limited to union dues, say $600 per year, and some small amounts for safety clothing and equipment, approximately $200 per year, for a total per year of $800. Contrast this to a conductor working a road job who lays-over 150 nights per year and incurs meal expenses of $20 per lay-over, or $3,000 per year, plus union dues of $1,200 and safety clothing and equipment of $200 per year, for a total per year of $4,400.

The majority of courts have also required deductions in the form of railroader-paid amounts for Tier I, Tier II, Medicare and other collectively bargained amounts. This legal issue is of significance in that traditional loss estimates without such deductions are noticeably higher. Similar to Social Security, Tier I deductions are equal to 6.20 percent of gross wages up to an annual maximum amount, $94,200 as of 2006. Also like Social Security, the railroad pays a matching amount. Tier II amounts as of 2005 are equal to 4.40 percent of gross wages up to an annual maximum amount, $69,900 as of 2006. Prior to 2005, the Tier II railroader contribution rate was equal to 4.90 percent. The reduction was made due to a projected surplus in the Railroad Retirement Pension Fund. Unlike Tier I, however, the railroad pays a much higher amount of the Tier II contribution, 12.60 percent as of 2006. Medicare is treated in the standard way and is equal to 1.45 percent of gross wages without an annual maximum amount. The collectively bargained amounts relate to employee cost-sharing of health, vision and dental insurance as agreed to late in 2003 by the United Transportation Union and the Brotherhood of Locomotive Engineers and the railroads; this sharing provides that the railroader will absorb a portion of future increases in the insurance costs borne by the railroads.

11.5 Retirement Benefits

Pension benefits for railroaders are administered by the Railroad Retirement Board and are paid under two programs: Tier I and Tier II. Both of these plans are defined-benefit plans. That is, the amount ultimately paid to the railroader upon retirement does not have a direct correlation to the amount paid into the plans by the railroader and by the railroad on his behalf, but rather is based upon the plan formulas which are based on a number of factors. Tier I is computed identically to Social Security. That is, it is based upon the monthly average of an individual's highest thirty-five years of indexed earnings, subject to the annual maximum. The index is used to convert earnings in previous years to their present-day equivalent. The Tier I benefit is then determined by multiplying a portion of this average by defined percentages in order to arrive at a monthly dollar amount. In 2005, a railroader would receive 90 percent of the first $626 of the monthly amount, 32 percent of the next $3,779, and 15 percent of the remainder. Tier II is a much simpler calculation. Upon retirement, a railroader will receive a monthly Tier II benefit equal to the average of his highest sixty months of service, subject to the annual maximum, multiplied by his number of service months, multiplied by 0.007. In both cases, the railroader needs to have a minimum of sixty months of service in order to qualify for a Tier I or Tier II benefit. Further, as it relates to Tier II benefits, a railroader may receive credited service months for military service provided he was a railroad employee both prior to and after his military service. Spouses of railroaders also receive a portion of the railroader earned benefit to the extent they are not offset by benefits they earned on their own behalf.

The calculation for Tier I and II benefit losses is the difference between two discrete computations: 1) the amount of annual Tier I and II benefits the railroader could have expected had he worked until his uninjured retirement age, discounted to present value through his expected date of death; and 2) the amount of annual Tier I and II benefits the railroader can expect upon retirement based upon his pre-injury actual and projected work, discounted to present value through his expected date of death.

11.6 Worklife Expectancy

The issue of worklife expectancy for an injured individual is the subject of much debate among forensic economists. This debate becomes more heated in railroad cases for a number of reasons. Because railroaders are covered under the Railroad Retirement Board and not the Social Security Administration, they have the option to retire with an unreduced benefit at age sixty provided they have thirty years of credited service in the railroad industry. This is different from their counterparts covered under Social Security who must wait until they are between ages sixty-five and sixty-seven for an unreduced benefit. Based upon this, many forensic economists hold that age sixty is the most appropriate retirement age for individuals with thirty years of service. Certainly there is some support for this position. The *22nd Actuarial Valuation,* as published by the Railroad Retirement Board, found that 60 percent of all those railroaders who reach age sixty with thirty years of service will retire. The question that arises, though, is what about the remaining 40 percent who do not retire at age sixty? Unfortunately, neither the Railroad Retirement Board data, nor statistical tables generated by other forensic economists based upon these data, address crucial issues such as the craft, earnings, and family situation of these individuals. Consequently, the forensic economist should evaluate this issue weighing the specifics of the injured railroader's situation against the statistics.

As we saw above, Tier I and Tier II retirement benefits have benefit ceilings based upon both the annual maximum covered earnings and the weighting of the Tier I calculation to first dollars. Consequently, higher earning individuals will realize a lower percentage of their pre-retirement income upon retirement than their lower earning counterparts. An example would be to assume the case of two railroaders retiring in 2006 at age sixty after forty years of railroad service. Railroader A earned $40,000 in his last full year of employment and similar adjusted wages during his previous forty years of work. Railroader B earned $100,000 in his last full year of employment and similar adjusted wages during his previous forty years of work. Upon retirement, Railroader A will receive Tier I and Tier II benefits equal to approximately $27,000 per year, or 67.50 percent of his final annual wages. Conversely, upon retirement, Railroader B will only receive Tier I and Tier II benefits equal to approximately $45,000 per year, or 45.00 percent of his final annual wages. All else being equal, Railroader B will certainly experience more of a lifestyle change based upon retiring at age sixty than Railroader A.

The railroader's family situation is also a crucial factor in determining worklife expectancy. While the same age and service requirements apply to the spousal portion of Tier I and Tier II benefits, often it is the case that the railroader and spouse are not the same age. In the case of a younger spouse, the railroader may choose to work beyond age sixty until his spouse reaches age sixty in order to receive an unreduced benefit for both him and his spouse. Further, younger spouses may be employed without an ability or desire to retire until they can receive an unreduced Social Security benefit at ages ranging between sixty-five and sixty-seven. Consequently, it should be apparent that the worklife expectancy of an injured railroader is impacted by a number of different factors, some of which are unique to the railroad industry. These factors must be weighed against the statistically average worklife in order to arrive at the most appropriate conclusion.

11.7 Summary

Railroad cases are unique both in the law governing the calculations and the nature of the employment system. Other cases involve unions and seniority-based employment, but because railroad cases are employee versus employer matters, significantly more information is available. The preceding is not meant to be a checklist for all issues that need addressing, or even of all issues that can be addressed in railroad cases. Each case is different. Rather, this chapter is a discussion of some of the particular factors facing forensic economists and attorneys in railroad matters. The CD accompanying this chapter includes several reference sources as well as a sample railroad case with earnings loss calculations.

Chapter 12

Punitive Damages

George A. Barrett, M.B.A., M.S.R.C., C.R.C., C.V.E. and
Michael L. Brookshire, Ph.D.

12.1 Introduction

In addition to compensatory damages, punitive damages are often sought by plaintiffs involved in various civil litigation matters. Punitive damages can be defined as an award provided by a court against a defendant as a deterrent or punishment to redress an egregious wrong perpetrated by the defendant. Although these two goals of punitive damages are similar, there is a distinction between deterrence and punishment.

The intention of deterrence is to discourage the defendant and other potential wrongdoers from committing similar behavior in the future. By deterring "bad" behavior, the court is attempting to prevent future legal actions related to similar conduct. A goal here is to limit the number of lawsuits filed by plaintiffs wronged by defendants by setting a precedent that such recklessness will be met with potentially harsh consequences. Both the actual defendant and potential defendants may be deterred.

Punishment, on the other hand, is specific to the actions of the tortfeasor and only considers the unique circumstances of the "bad act" and the amount necessary to penalize the defendant for committing the behavior. The ultimate goal of punishment is not to deter future behavior by establishing a precedent for the judgment of such wrongs. It would be fallacy to ignore the deterring features of punishment as deterrence could easily be a secondary effect of such levies against a defendant. However, it must be remembered that the overall goal of punishment is to simply discipline the defendant without regard for how occurrences of future "bad behavior" are affected, either negatively or positively, by the imposition of punitive damages.

Although punitive damages have a long history in the American legal system, it is interesting that the use of expert testimony has been infrequent for such a potentially large component of total damages. This seems to be the case for both the plaintiff and defense sides of litigation. Traditionally, expert witnesses have only provided basic financial information to the trier or fact. For example, a certified public accountant may have testified on the financial condition and performance of a defendant company. This information may have been used by the plaintiff side to illustrate the vast wealth of a defendant corporation, often with an underlying emphasis that the alleged "bad behavior" earned or preserved this prosperity. On the other hand, testimony may have been solicited by the defense side to demonstrate the financial reality of a defendant struggling to stay afloat amid the competitive pressures of her industry. For the most part, forensic accountants, and to a lesser extent forensic economists, have testified on punitive damages without referring to punitive damages. Instead, this testimony has been a basic recital of audited financial statements.

12.2 Alternative Approaches

Several strategies have been developed by legal counsel on the most effective presentation of financial data to affect the amount of a punitive damages award. Plaintiff attorneys will be quick to point to the corporation's balance sheet. Beginning at the top of the standard balance sheet there will be a comprehensive listing of assets, which will include physical and financial holdings. Of course, leading the list will be the asset most readily understandable by the trier of fact, cash. Defense attorneys may also be attracted to the balance sheet if the corporation is heavily debt laden, resulting in a decreased net worth of the entity. Either side may see a benefit in presenting the historical financial performance of the company as recorded by the income (also referred to as the profit and loss) statement. Obviously, the plaintiff side will wish to emphasize the profitability of the entity while the defense will attempt to convey poor financial performance.

There are many issues of strategy. Plaintiffs may wish to convey recent trends of the defendant corporation that may be unfavorably perceived, such as large rounds of employee layoffs while the compensation of executives increases. It can also be anticipated that the plaintiff will communicate the intricate details of the alleged misconduct in an attempt to portray such behavior as being "especially egregious," which might be an exception to the single-digit punitive damages multiplier limit. Defendants might pursue similar subjective methods by introducing into evidence the number of employees, average wage paid, or any other statistic that may encourage the trier of fact to be more sympathetic toward the corporation. In addition, the defendant may wish to convey that public knowledge of the alleged misconduct may lead to a decrease in product sales resulting in an overall reduction in profitability with corresponding reductions in equity, i.e., lower stock prices. Such "reputation effects" might lead to duplication of punitive damages as the corporation will pay an award to the plaintiff and subsequently realize additional losses. Strategies and tactics aside, the courts all seem to agree that when it comes to punitive damages, the defendant corporation should not be destroyed as a going concern by the award with the Due Process Clause of the Fourteenth Amendment to the U.S. Constitution cited as the reason for this precaution.

This requirement of punitive damages to not destroy the company seems to have prevented a great deal of expert testimony on the specific amount necessary to either deter or punish the defendant. It seems that it was all too easy for financial experts and even corporate managers and officers to testify about financial generalities and then allow the jury to determine an amount to award. Unfortunately, most juries lack the training and experience to agree on the specific amount of punitive damages necessary, below which there is no deterring effect or beyond which the corporation may be destroyed. Social scientists, and even more specifically economists, seem well suited for providing assistance on when these thresholds are met or exceeded.

12.3 Judicial Guidelines

Economists providing expert testimony on the specific amount of punitive damages would be well advised to understand the court-prescribed factors for jury consideration in determining an appropriate amount of punitive damages. The most often cited U.S. Supreme Court decisions regarding punitive damages are *BMW of North America, Inc. v. Gore* (1996) and *State Farm Mutual Automobile Insurance Co. v. Campbell* (2003), in which the Court directly and indirectly provided five of these factors for juries to consider in determining the amount of punitive damages. These factors are often used at the trial court level as well as by appellate courts across the nation when punitive damages issues are being decided. The factors are (1) the reprehensibility of the defendant's conduct; (2) disparity between the potential harm suffered by the plaintiff to the award; (3) comparisons to comparable punitive awards and civil penalties for similar misconduct; (4) apportioning the scope of punitive awards to business activity within the political subdivision in which the specific case is being litigated; and (5) prevention of excessive punitive awards which are greater than nine times actual damages. Of course, state courts have instituted supplemental factors that do not seem to contradict the federal guidelines. For example, the profits obtained through the alleged misconduct may be disgorged from the defendant as a minimum of punishment.

Although the courts have provided these guidelines for juries, no preferential weighting for the individual factors has been given. This has led to some degree of confusion because factors one, three, and four appear to be punishment based, with factors two and five appearing to be more related to the deterrence purpose. Because of this, separate analyses are needed to present an opinion on the appropriate amount of punitive damages.

Applications of these methods to a sample case may be beneficial for better understanding. For the purposes of punitive damages, let us assume that the defendant in the case is an international manufacturer of agricultural products. Consideration of the jury factors is important when attempting to provide expert opinions on punitive damages.

12.4 Optimal Deterrence

Let us begin by considering a deterrence model. Beyond the basic definition of deterrence provided in this text, it is important to understand the concept of "optimal deterrence." Optimal deterrence occurs when the dollar benefits of a chosen level of product or service safety (for example) and the costs of providing that level of safety are equal to each other from the perspective of a business firm. In this scenario, society will not desire the firm to move beyond this level of safety because of the increased costs required to increase the safeness of the product or services offered. A practical example is the perfectly safe automobile in which it may be possible for an automobile manufacturer to construct an indestructible car. While perfectly safe for its operator and occupants, such a car would require development and manufacturing costs exceeding what society would be willing to pay. The solution is for society to balance its desire for safety with what it is willing to pay the manufacturer for an acceptable level of risk.

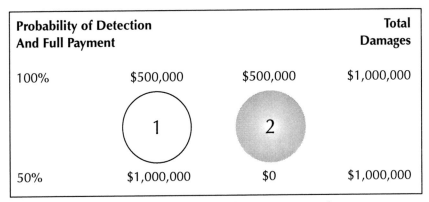

Probability of Detection And Full Payment			Total Damages
100%	$500,000	$500,000	$1,000,000
	1	2	
50%	$1,000,000	$0	$1,000,000

Figure 12.1 Effects of the probability of detecting two future occurrences of defendant misconduct resulting in actual damages

In the sample case shown in Figure 12.1, assume that total damages that actually occurred in each incidence of the defendant's alleged misconduct were $500,000 in present value. Deterrence theory is applicable when it is believed that similar misconduct may not be detected, with the negligent or guilty parties escaping the responsibility of paying the entire compensatory damages inflicted by their misbehavior. In our example, a 100 percent probability of detection would mean that all compensatory damages would be paid with each occurrence of this misconduct, and no amount of punitive damages would be necessary for optimal deterrence. The reality of the situation is that a 100 percent probability of detection is unlikely. Instead, let us assume that each harm from misconduct is detected only 50 percent of the time. Given that the defendant only has a one in two chance of being detected and paying compensatory damages, the defendant must pay an additional $500,000 in punitive damages to make up for the one chance in two of not being detected. The direct punitive multiplier of actual damages can be found by the formula $(1 - p) \div p$, where p equals the probability of detection and full payment for harm. Therefore, in our example, the sum of 1 minus 0.50 divided by 0.50 equals 1.00, so the punitive damages amount is one times the actual damages in the case.

The logic behind this theory of deterrence is that the defendant must pay for all actual harm attributed to its misconduct when it is actually detected and under our assumption of a 50 percent probability of detection, this only happens one half of the time. So, when caught, the defendant must not only pay actual damages for its misbehavior but also make up for the times when misbehavior was not detected. Figure 12.1 shows that the optimal deterrence model forces a defendant to consider, and bear, the full social costs from its chosen level of safety—$1 million.

Under this model, the amount of punitive damages varies with the probability of detection. Following the optimal deterrence punitive damages multiplier formula described above, the relationship between detection and the multiple of punitive damages is summarized in Table 12.1. In keeping with the guidance provided by the U.S. Supreme Court in *State Farm*, you see that a punitive damages multiplier greater than nine is only calculated with a corresponding probability of detection less than 10 percent. At the other extreme, (p) values moving from 50 percent to 100 percent mean punitive damages multiples moving from 1.0 to zero. With the significance of the value of the (p), its determination may be the most difficult aspect of calculating punitive damages under the deterrence model.

Because of this difficulty, economists should expect to utilize the expertise of supporting professionals such as actuaries, attorneys, investigators, and so on who may understand the likelihood of similar behavior and its detection. Or, the determination of a "p" value is simply left to the trier of fact.

Table 12.1

Probability of Detection/Punishment and Punitive to Compensatory Damages Multiplier

Probability of Detection and Full Payment of Actual Damages (p)	Multiple of Punitive to Compensatory Damages $(1 - p) \div p$
1%	99.0
5%	19.0
10%	9.0
20%	4.0
30%	2.3
40%	1.5
50%	1.0
60%	0.7
70%	0.4
80%	0.3
90%	0.1
100%	0.0

12.5 Punish But Not Destroy

An alternative to the deterrence model is to provide a specific dollar amount to punish the tortfeasor for the misconduct. Only recently have attempts been made through expert testimony to assist the trier of fact in determining the amount necessary to punish a defendant. As previously described, expert testimony on this topic has traditionally been limited to the recital of key corporate financial data. Pursuing this strategy, attorneys limited any interpretation of what these numbers might mean for a punitive damages verdict. Instead, they have left these decisions to juries after simply providing the information. Sources of this information have been income statements demonstrating financial performance over time, the balance sheet illustrating financial position at a given time, and perhaps the statement of cash flows indicating the sums of cash the business is accustomed to receiving and dispersing over a period of time. Obviously, plaintiffs will seek to introduce evidence through testimony that the defendant is abundantly wealthy and can easily pay a punitive damages award. Similarly, the defense will attempt to convey the inability of the accused to pay punitive damages without ceasing to exist. The jury is left to ascertain the degree of reprehensibility of the alleged misconduct and somehow to translate this into a dollar amount of punishment which will not go so far as destroying the defendant company.

A forensic economist can discuss dollar amounts that might destroy a defendant company, based upon long-established and generally accepted economic theory. Microeconomic theory states that a firm will only continue operations if it can earn a so-called "normal" profit. The "normal" rate of profit is the bare minimum the shareholders will accept before redistributing the capital allocated to the firm to alternative investment opportunities that are more lucrative. For example, an investor in a "large cap" business may expect a 10 percent annual return on his investment. This basic level of required return is often labeled the "hurdle rate." Because this rate of return is very similar to the rate of return on publicly traded securities, informed investors will remove their financial interests from a particular endeavor when the rate of return consistently dips below the expected 10 percent level.

Corporations strive to earn profits that will be above the "normal" level. The metric establishing the "hurdle rate" for a corporation is difficult to precisely ascertain. Individual firms exist within unique industries and the uncertainties of operating within these parameters dictate that differing rates of return be realized. As a rule, the more risky a business venture, the greater the rate of return should be as a compensatory reward for bearing the risk. Because of this direct relationship between risk and return, individual "hurdle rates" are intricate matters to determine. However, if a shareholder is aware that a basic level of return is available across all industries, then she would surely redistribute her capital to other ventures if the rate of return in a chosen investment consistently performed below this economy-wide standard. The tasks thus become the identification of an appropriate "hurdle rate" and contemplating the length of time that an investor will tolerate her capital returning less than this amount.

Timing issues in forensic economics are often best handled by providing the trier of fact with a continuum. With alternative opinions related to when the capital can be expected to flee, the jury will have several options for rendering a final decision. Then the remaining variable is the hurdle rate used to ascertain the "normal" profit. Once the "hurdle rate" is established, it is possible to calculate the amount of punitive damages that a company will be able to pay, beyond which the entity will be destroyed as capital flees to better investment opportunities. This is because an amount of profits beyond the "normal" level will be available to pay any punitive award. This "excess" profit can be used by the corporation to pay the award, leaving enough profit to maintain the "normal" level. This highlights a difference between deterrence and punishment. In deterrence, emphasis is placed upon both the losses sustained by the plaintiff (actual damages) and the behavior of the defendant (the ratio of punitive to actual damages). In punishment, the focus is solely on the defendant.

In Table 12.2, financial data from the defendant corporation in the sample case are presented. Here, the corporation has estimated a 15 percent annual rate of return on equity with a noted minimum "hurdle rate" of 10 percent, which yields a mathematical difference of 5 percent identified as the excess internal rate of return. Applying these rates to the stockholders' equity yields profits above the "normal" level, meaning that the corporation could afford to pay $150 million per year in punitive damages before investors would be expected to flee and invest in other opportunities, destroying the business.

The length of time that investors would tolerate paying $150 million per year in punitive damages is uncertain; therefore, a continuum is provided with a cumulative column. It is anticipated that testimony will be heard both on the egregiousness of the defendant's behavior, along with how likely capital flight is to occur. The trier of fact may weigh these opinions and then levy an amount of punitive damages commensurate with the amount of time expected to be sustainable by investors. This way, the corporation will adequately cover its liability for damages and yet remain a viable entity. However, it must be remembered that in *BMW v. Gore,* the U.S. Supreme Court stated that it is necessary to apportion any national financial data to the appropriate political subdivision in which the tort occurred. U.S.-wide values on financial statements would be translated to values reflecting the defendants' activities within the particular state.

Table 12.2
Calculation of a Punishment Continuum for the Defendant Corporation
2006–2010

Year	Stockholder's Equity	Estimated Internal Rate of Return	Estimated Internal Rate of Return Net Income Before Tax	Normal Internal Rate of Return	Normal Internal Rate of Return Net Income Before Tax
2006	$3 Billion	15%	$450 Million	10%	$300 Million
2007	$3 Billion	15%	$450 Million	10%	$300 Million
2008	$3 Billion	15%	$450 Million	10%	$300 Million
2009	$3 Billion	15%	$450 Million	10%	$300 Million
2010	$3 Billion	15%	$450 Million	10%	$300 Million

Year	Excess Internal Rate of Return	Excess Internal Rate of Return Net Income Before Tax	Discount Factor (10%)	Present Value	Cumulative Present Value
2006	5%	$150 Million	1.0000	$150 Million	$150 Million
2007	5%	$150 Million	0.9091	$136 Million	$286 Million
2008	5%	$150 Million	0.8265	$124 Million	$410 Million
2009	5%	$150 Million	0.7513	$113 Million	$523 Million
2010	5%	$150 Million	0.6830	$102 Million	$625 Million

In the sample case, the defendant corporation is a manufacturer that markets its products throughout the nation. As such, its operations in the state in which the alleged misconduct took place represent only a fraction of its total. Determining the proper method of apportioning corporate data to the state level may be difficult. Ideally, corporate financial data would be available identifying the revenues generated by operations in that state, or even more desirable would be the percentage of profits derived by those state-specific sales. The national profits can then be apportioned in accordance with the *BMW v. Gore* decision. It may be found that state-specific financial data are not available for the defendant corporation. In such events, proxies such as number of franchised locations, or even population, may be utilized. Let us assume that in the sample case, sufficient data are available to apportion profits to the state level. Assume that 5 percent of profits were derived from the sales of the corporation's products to consumers in the state in which the sample case is being litigated. It may be necessary to then apportion all data accordingly.

Therefore, financial values in Table 12.3 are 5 percent of those presented in Table 12.2. Thusly, apportionment at 5 percent results in a reduction of the five-year cumulative present value of excess profits from $625 million to $31.3 million. It should be noted that national values may also be "scaled" to reflect a particular product or service line from a company with multiple products or services.

There are basically two purposes of punitive damages. If deterrence of future incidences of the alleged misconduct is desired, the theory of optimal deterrence should be applied to the case specifics to determine the amount of punitive damages necessary to meet this goal. By first calculating compensatory, or actual, damages and then determining the probability that such misbehavior will be detected in the future, the punitive damages multiplier can be used to quantify a specific amount of punitive damages. If it is the goal to punish the defendant for misconduct, the amount of punitive damages cannot be beyond the sum that would result in the entity continuing as a going concern. By ascertaining the historical financial performance of the defendant and comparing this result to the expected performance of similar entities, excess profits may be identified which may be utilized for the payment of a punitive damages award.

Table 12.3
Calculation of a Punishment Continuum for the Defendant Corporation
2006–2010 Apportioned at Five Percent of Corporate Totals

Year	Stockholder's Equity	Estimated Internal Rate of Return	Estimated Internal Rate of Return Net Income Before Tax	Normal Internal Rate of Return	Normal Internal Rate of Return Net Income Before Tax
2006	$150 Million	15%	$22.5 Million	10%	$15 Million
2007	$150 Million	15%	$22.5 Million	10%	$15 Million
2008	$150 Million	15%	$22.5 Million	10%	$15 Million
2009	$150 Million	15%	$22.5 Million	10%	$15 Million
2010	$150 Million	15%	$22.5 Million	10%	$15 Million

Year	Excess Internal Rate of Return	Excess Internal Rate of Return Net Income Before Tax	Discount Factor (10%)	Present Value	Cumulative Present Value
2006	5%	$7.5 Million	1.0000	$7.5 Million	$7.5 Million
2007	5%	$7.5 Million	0.9091	$6.8 Million	$14.3 Million
2008	5%	$7.5 Million	0.8265	$6.2 Million	$20.5 Million
2009	5%	$7.5 Million	0.7513	$5.6 Million	$26.2 Million
2010	5%	$7.5 Million	0.6830	$5.1 Million	$31.3 Million

12.6 The *State Farm v. Campbell* Exception

Practitioners should always be mindful of relevant legal opinions concerning punitive damages. Although mathematical formulae exist to calculate punitive damages, exceptions may exist precluding their use in a pure sense. For example, although a punitive damages multiplier may be determined based upon an optimal deterrence model, the application of that multiplier may be adjusted upward or downward due to the specific facts of the case. It may be found that unique circumstances existed, which caused actual damages to be very low compared to what potential damages could have been. For example, the "lucky tortfeasor" may have caused an accident to occur; however, the accident took place at a time when relatively few people and their property were present, such as in the collapse of a city parking garage early on Sunday morning as opposed to the collapse happening on Monday afternoon. Actual personal and property damage was minimized because the defendant was "lucky" by the timing of the occurrence. Since the collapse of a parking garage will hardly go unnoticed, the effective probability of detection will yield a punitive damages multiplier on the lower end of the spectrum. Since actual damages were "luckily" small, resulting punitive damages as provided by the multiplier formula may be insufficient to optimally deter future misconduct. In such cases, a higher multiplier may be required and/or an estimate of likely or probable actual damages may be made. This is the exception to the single-digit multiplier cap of *State Farm v. Campbell* (2003).

12.7 Disgorgement of Profits and Comparable Civil Fines

An additional method of punitive damages estimation is the removal of profit gained by the defendant through the alleged misconduct. A punitive amount should be in excess of profits to a defendant from "bad acts." A difficulty in quantifying the amount of profits to be disgorged from the defendant is the isolation of profits gained by the defendant from an alleged "bad act" or set of "bad acts." Generally, company financial data, and profits specifically, are not disaggregated in company financial statements by punitive-related groupings or for the relevant political subdivision. Nevertheless, disgorgement of illicit gains is a potential method of punitive damages estimation.

Another factor, which has been suggested for jury consideration in evaluating the appropriate amount of punitive damages, is the amount of civil fines for similar conduct. Both the *BMW v. Gore* and *State Farm v. Campbell* decisions by the U.S. Supreme Court mention the applicability of comparable civil fines as a benchmark for punitive damages. Such benchmarks are often codified by the relevant statutory law and may be found with the assistance of legal counsel.

12.8 Summary and Conclusion

Historically, expert testimony has been employed sparingly by both the plaintiff and defense sides of cases to assist the trier of fact in determining the amount of punitive damages necessary to either punish or deter a defendant for committing misconduct. This lack of assistance has often led to discouraging results, high rates of appeal, and an overall inefficiency of the court system for both plaintiffs and defendants. Increasingly, federal and state guidelines are sufficiently clear that economic analysis can provide effective guidance to triers of fact in determining appropriate amounts of punitive damages. Forensic economists may use such analyses to present evidence regarding the specific amount of punitive damages necessary to deter or punish without destroying the company. New methods of damages calculations, such as those presented in this chapter, should prove useful to jurors in making a determination of punitive damages.

In the compact disc chapter, extensive references are provided for those who wish to further pursue this topic. A glossary of terminology relevant to the litigation of punitive damage amounts is provided. The sample case of Jackie Travis, which has been carried throughout the CD, is tailored to the topic of punitive damages and the analyses described in this chapter. Finally, sample testimony segments are provided.

Chapter 13

Inside the Mediation Experience: Proof, Practice, and Preparation

Howard H. Vogel, Esq.

Synopsis

13.1 Introduction

This chapter is one mediator's look at this wonderful process. While this is not exactly a Mediation 101 course, it is intended to be a rather basic overview of the practical approach to the use of and preparation for the process of dispute resolution in this manner. Most of the other chapters of this thoughtful and practical treatise are designed to assist you in sharpening your tools in evaluating and presenting damages. This chapter describes one place within the law where those tools can be put to valuable use.

Where did this mediation thing get its start? We can look back to 1976 to find substantial evidence of the foundation for what has become the frequent and popular use of mediation for the resolution of civil disputes in our country. At that time, U.S. Supreme Court Chief Justice Warren Burger issued a challenge to the American legal profession to find alternatives to trials and means by which the crush upon the American court system could be remedied. He thought there was too much litigation and the capacity of the judicial system was being sorely tested. Courts were crowded and often justice delayed was justice denied. Harvard Law School professor Frank Sander was called upon to deliver a presentation at the 1976 Roscoe Pound Conference on the causes of popular dissatisfaction with the administration of justice. He titled his remarks "Varieties of Dispute Processing." His words captured the imagination of many, including the American Bar Association. Certain of his concepts became known as the "multi-door courthouse." Mediation became the most popular and prevalent alternative dispute resolution mechanism. In the thirty years that followed the teaching of mediation, the process of mediation, and its styles and theories, has evolved and will continue to do so. The mediation process we know today has formed within the second half of the past thirty years of development.

Various centers for conflict resolution have emerged across the country, including the Strauss Institute for Dispute Resolution at the Pepperdine University Law School in Malibu, California, and the Program on Negotiation at Harvard University in Cambridge, Massachusetts. At the time of this writing, Lipscomb University in Nashville, Tennessee, is going forward with its Center for Conflict Management. Today's law students have the opportunity to learn about the mediation process and mediation advocacy as they prepare to enter the conflicts within the American society and legal environment.

13.2 Three Styles of Mediation

Although the ADR movement in its most visible forms dates back to 1976, the more significant work in the development of various styles for mediation has occurred within the last fifteen to twenty years. The three principal styles are referred to as evaluative, facilitative and transformative.

In the evaluative mode, the mediator assists the parties with her experience in assessing how similar cases might progress through the legal system with the focus on various disposition dynamics and their relationship to a likely or potential end result. This might include offering opinions regarding witness credibility issues, damage evaluations, legal theories or defenses, or the practical implications associated with jurisdiction and venue. Lawyers often ask for frank evaluation and occasionally a party will directly request it. The capacity of the mediator to engage in the evaluation might relate to the rules or regulations imposed upon the mediator in a particular state or jurisdiction.

In the facilitative mode, the mediator seeks to assist the parties in advancing the discussions and negotiation within the best possible light. The mediator serves as an enabler, assisting the parties in "putting their best foot forward."

Transformative style mediators primarily focus upon recognition and empowerment issues that might be in conflict with the potential for resolution. Often, one party may feel at a disadvantage in the negotiation. This may result from a lack of experience with the legal system, a lack of knowledge regarding the complex subtleties or circumstances underlying the dispute, or a retiring personality trait. Certainly, lawyers for such parties are valuable supporters of their clients' best interests. If a client participant is too encumbered by such issues, she might either refuse to participate or fail to participate in a meaningful way. The mediator can be of great assistance in explaining the means and opportunities at hand, as well as the benefits of the confidential mediation process. The mediator can assist the parties in achieving communication and negotiation "on the same page" or upon the same plateau. Then, the parties are more likely to achieve an enduring resolution that is premised upon a solid foundation of thoughtful analysis and understanding.

Effective mediation may be seen as often requiring employment of aspects of each of these three styles of mediation.

13.3 Role of the Mediator

In addition to the above stylistic approaches, the mediator has the potential to serve as a very important participant in meaningful conversation about the opportunities for resolution. The mediator is almost always the last person to arrive within the dispute and is statistically likely to be present for the last day of it. While the parties, their counsel, consultants, and experts may have labored for years within the controversy, the time for participation of the mediator may be as short as weeks and rarely more than a few months. It is a unique manner of service and an extraordinarily important one.

Sometimes, the role of the mediator is simply to keep the parties within a sequence of meaningful conversations. Only the engaged neutral can accomplish this and the patience of the mediator is a necessity. Sometimes the role of the mediator is to help the parties explore opportunity at the fringe. Sometimes it is referred to as "thinking outside the box" or "pushing the envelope." A mediator can suggest things that parties and their counsel might never ponder. It is not "always about the money."

13.4 Role of the Mediation Advocate

Years ago, lawyers walked into mediations and acted as if the jury had been empanelled and the trial was commencing. There is a distinct difference between trial advocacy and mediation advocacy, just as there is a recognized distinction for appellate advocacy. As the use of mediation has increased, the subtleties associated with the distinctions have evolved.

The lawyer, as mediation advocate, has several tasks and objectives which can improve the chances for a successful resolution within the mediation process. Before the mediation day the lawyer reviews the file in detail, if only to prepare a narrative confidential position statement to provide to the mediator. It is important that the lawyer meet with the client and client representatives before the day of the mediation, to review the respective positions of the parties, discuss the anticipated approach for negotiation, and prepare for what positions and approaches the opponents might utilize.

If discovery needs to be supplemented in advance of the mediation, it should be. Time and opportunity can be wasted if the day of the mediation is the first time that material information is provided to the opposition. This prohibits a substantive analysis of material information in advance of the negotiation and could impede progress or stall it out entirely. While it is customary to provide position statements to the mediator for her eyes only, it is often advisable for the attorneys to exchange some information before the mediation. That information can lead to meaningful pre-mediation dialogue among counsel and occasionally with the mediator.

The best work that the disputant's attorney might do is provide a thoughtful synthesis of the case, with commentary about the good, the bad, and the ugly within the confidential position statements supplied to the mediator. Most mediators are not interested in reading all the depositions, but excerpts can be helpful. The same goes for documents relating to the controversy, with the possible exception of narrative reports of key expert witnesses.

It is important to let the mediator know if there are any issues, circumstances, personalities, or other things or matters that might impede the opportunities for resolution on mediation day. Some mention of this in the confidential mediation statement or a phone call to the mediator can pay great dividends after the mediation commences. An experienced and resourceful mediator can help get past the rough spots on occasion.

As the focus of this treatise is the realm of economic damages, it is important to permit the mediator to review reports of the forensic economist in advance of the day of the mediation. The mediator will likely know of the economist, through either prior mediation experience or litigation involvement. The mediator will likely know to look for jurisdiction-specific issues, such as a consumption factor in a wrongful death analysis or variations in mathematical assumptions, used by different economists. An experienced mediator can quickly discern if there are variances with custom in the development of the reports of forensic economists.

As the mediation advocate prepares for the day of the mediation, thoughtful consideration should be given to what manner of presentation will be made in the opening session. The prevalent method for personal injury and wrongful death mediation incorporates an opening session, followed by negotiation within caucus sessions. It seems that from one legal community to the other, styles for presentation within the opening session vary. Some attorneys choose to welcome all participants and affirm the benefit of mediation as a vehicle for meaningful conversation. Other attorneys use the opening session to incorporate a manner of mediation advocacy, outlining pertinent facts, damage theories, outcomes in similar trials, and so on. Electronic presentation media have worked their way into such sessions and can be powerful illustrators of fact and position. In some cases, mediation advocates choose to aggressively challenge the other side with dramatic presentations that may graphically illustrate extraordinary events, loss, or potentiality for outcomes. Delicate moments can follow. Early termination of the mediation can be at risk. The mediation advocacy of the recipient can be tested. Nothing much seems surprising anymore and the experienced mediator knows that there are usually reasons why such drama was invoked or was necessary. Beyond that, it can be a form of venting that is usually psychologically necessary by one participant or another if meaningful negotiations are to follow.

On the defense side, most mediation advocates find themselves not wanting to create a chill or to act in a manner that might lessen the opportunity for resolution. The defense side mediation advocates often speak of coins having two sides and the need to keep an open mind.

13.5 Convening the Mediation

The convening of the mediation begins before everyone arrives on mediation day. It involves the scheduling process and it begins the education of the mediator regarding the substance of the controversy. In addition to the mechanics of when, where, and who, it can be the opportunity for an early focus upon aspects of the dispute, which might need a little special attention.

On some occasions, the parties who called to schedule the mediation take the opportunity to speak with the mediator and address various concerns. There may be issues regarding where the mediation will be held and the need for neutral turf. This could be a signal that there have been communication issues, power impact disparities, or other concerns during the pendancy of the litigation. This is not always the case, as some counsel prefer the neutral ground start for discussing resolution.

Some disputes deserve pre-mediation conferencing. Different parties will ask for it on occasion. The mediator may suggest it. A pre-mediation conference may be convened with only counsel for one of the disputing parties or with the disputing party present. It is a good time to educate the mediator regarding the complexity of the dispute, any personality issues and the potential framework for resolution. If one party requests such a pre-mediation conference, the mediator should advise the other side and offer them the same opportunity.

After telephone calls or letters have been exchanged regarding the details for the actual scheduling of mediation, the scheduling and engagement letter is prepared and sent. This is an opportunity for the mediator to get some advance sense of what the dynamics for the session might be.

The following are points that a mediator might use in a scheduling letter:

- The mediator asks that the parties or their representatives be present and that they have authority to resolve the dispute. If the mediation is proceeding as a part of a court's process with a state or local rule applicable, the presence of the clients and the authority capacities may be driven by the provisions of such a rule. Occasionally, questions regarding "authority and authority to resolve the case" become difficult, thorny, precarious, or terminal issues.

- The mediator might suggest that the mediation day begin with a joint session with the parties and their counsel in the same room. They will be forewarned that each attorney will be asked to describe the lawsuit from the point of view of her client and that there will be no time limit for this general discussion. Ten to fifteen minutes per party is usually adequate to provide a fair overview, but if more time is necessary, that does not create a problem. They will be told that the mediator may ask questions during the opening session, in an effort to clarify or define the issues. This description is not included to educate the attorney, but to assist the attorney in educating her client. In the early days of mediation, many lawyers needed the explanation for how the session would begin and progress. Mediation has come a long way and few attorneys need this insight now. However, there are differing styles for commencing a mediation and inviting participation and commentary within the joint session. The mediator may adapt to the styles of the attorneys.

- After the opening general session, there will be private conversations with counsel and clients in separate rooms. The private conversations are for the purpose of continuing, and in some cases beginning, the talk about the matters of interest. Such caucus sessions are necessary for frank and candid discussion about the elements, substance, and settlement opportunities associated with personal injury and wrongful death litigation. It is also suggested that circumstances may develop such that resuming a general session might be of benefit to the parties sometime during the day. Such references are included to enable the attorneys to advise their clients prior to the mediation not to be surprised by such a suggestion or any other aspect of the mediation process. While resuming a general session is not common, there are circumstances in which an important set of facts or developments might best be communicated by one party to the other face-to-face.

- The parties are advised that there may be circumstances wherein the mediator requests the opportunity to speak with the attorneys privately and without their respective clients being present. The attorney can discuss this potentiality with the client before the day of the mediation. On the slight chance that the client might be suspicious, it is good for the client to know that it occasionally happens, and that it is a permissible part of the process.
- It is suggested that the mediation should be informal and without significant structure. The parties should feel comfortable, free to express their views as they see fit, and comfortable in listening to views expressed by others. Some mediations are more formal than others. However, it is important for the disputants to understand in the very beginning that a mediation is not a trial and that attitudes and demeanor are very different.
- Some mediators prefer to know very little about the dispute before walking in to meet and greet the disputants on the day of the mediation. It is my belief that the mediator can best perform if the mediator is given a reasonable opportunity to learn about the controversy and give it some thought. It is suggested that the parties provide me with certain information. If they wish to submit it for "my eyes only," that is their choice. Suggested categories are as follows:

  a. Identity of the parties, insurance carriers, participating claims representatives, and any contractual or statutory subrogation interest or liens.
  b. A statement of the basic facts and the history of the case, including the date of the subject event, the date the suit was filed, the pending trial date, the discovery status, and a list of the depositions for use of evidence that have been taken.
  c. A brief statement of the basis for the conflict and what you would expect to be resolved.
  d. Your opinions of the strengths and weaknesses of the respective positions of the parties.
  e. A brief statement or description of any unusual or significant points of law or medicine, if applicable.
  f. A description of any key or significant documents that you believe are relevant to the dispute.
  g. Calculations of any special damages, whether disputed or not.
  h. Summaries of the opinions of any experts that are anticipated to be used at trial.

      i. A brief history of settlement discussions up to the time of the mediation.

      j. A copy of any applicable order of reference to mediation.

      k. A description of any factors or circumstances, which you believe might impede settlement discussions.

- It is important to know who will attend the mediation and what their relationship to the dispute is. The party's synopsis of the dispute, its history, the strengths and weaknesses of both sides, and the factual, legal, medical and damage foundations are important. It may be the same dispute, but often the parties address these categories of information in significantly different ways and with differing opinions regarding various strengths and weaknesses.

- While it may seem elemental, getting the parties to commit to things like subrogation interests, liens, special damage calculations, and so on, is very important to the prospects for successful resolution. The unknown subrogation interest, revealed on the day of the mediation, can create the chance for early impasse. A fresh list of medical expenses and bills revealed on the day of the mediation can trigger the same thing. The mediation day revelation of the report of a forensic economist can likewise cause an immediate stall. Such critical information should be exchanged by the parties well in advance of the mediation. If the parties have negotiated before the day of the mediation, tell the mediator. Sometimes, settlement discussions have a lack of formality and one side may have thought that something was proposed, when actually it was not. This results in the parties not being on the same page walking into the mediation. It is far better for the mediator to be aware of this in advance and ready to assist in smoothing such circumstances, if possible.

- Although it varies from state to state, it is important for the mediator to know whether the mediation is occurring by court order or if it has been scheduled as a private mediation. If court ordered, the local rule for mediation in that jurisdiction may have reporting requirements for the mediator. Often, the order of reference to mediation will set out deadlines for reporting and scheduling.

- On occasion, there are undercurrents or circumstances, which, if known to the mediator, would assist in the conversations that follow. It is a good thing to let the mediator know in advance if there are any unusual personalities, unusual procedural developments or any facts or circumstances which might impede settlement discussions on mediation day. Such information is usually communicated for the eyes of the mediator only, but it can be extremely important information. It is good to know where the mines are, before beginning the thoughtful stroll through the minefield.

- It is suggested that the parties submit their information in a manner convenient for them. This could be by e-mail attachment or traditional letter. Occasionally, they provide a DVD that includes segments of deposition testimony, day-in-the-life video footage, or relevant photographs.

- The attorneys are reminded and asked to confirm with their clients that the statements and information transmitted to the mediator are to be kept in confidence unless specifically advised to the contrary. Statements made before, within, or in connection with the mediation are considered to be confidential.

13.6 The Opening Session

The opening session of a mediation is the beginning of meaningful conversation. It is a time for the parties to meet and greet. You can find articles that have been written about the important psychology of this commencement. Commentators speak about the shape of the table, who sits where, and whether flowers will be in the room. Remember that first impressions are important. Power relationships and attitudes are often evident immediately.

After everyone is seated, the mediator might provide a ten to twelve minute introduction. These remarks are often customized on the fly. It is an opportunity to introduce the mediator, as the last person to arrive in the dispute, and to explain the value and importance of the mediation process. The participants may give nodding acknowledgment around the room. The mediator looks for evidence of non-verbal communication that may otherwise be good or bad. If the message is resonating, there is usually some unspoken evidence. The lawyers for the parties are offered the chance to make their presentations. The mediator should follow the flow that the parties establish, as the conversation among them continues. Sometimes, the mediator is asked in advance for a preference regarding opening sessions. My preference is for a positive substantive conversation among the parties. Often that is difficult to accomplish and the attorneys choose to limit their remarks to general greetings of good faith and hope for resolution. If the parties prefer to simply say very little and proceed into the caucus sessions, that is fine with me.

If the parties choose to enter into substantive discussion, occasionally the mediator will ask questions. If the parties choose to limit their remarks to hello and let's get to work, the mediator might not ask questions, as this approach may be their way of requesting that substantive discussions stay in caucus.

13.7 The Caucus

After the general session, the parties take a few minutes to regroup in different caucus rooms. The first private session for each party is very important. Sometimes, statements made in the opening session need a response or an explanation. This is an opportunity for some venting, in addition to critical analysis. The most important thing done by a mediator in the first caucus may be to listen, rather than ask questions. The parties need very few questions from the mediator in order to begin their own expression of the things that really matter: their needs, their perceptions, the dispute, the disputants, their lawyers, and an opportunity that the day might bring.

For the mediator, the first caucus is a unique opportunity. It is important for the disputants to get certain things off of their chests and to come to grips with not only the basis for the dispute, but the realistic potential for resolution. While all of this might not be manifest in the first caucus, the seeds usually are.

Experienced mediators know that the processing aspect of mediation is extraordinarily important. Very few cases resolve within a couple of hours and only several exchanges of proposals for settlement. I tend to speak of the exchanges as innings and for me most mediations are twelve to twenty innings in length. Each inning brings opportunity, as the levels of awareness increase and the parties continue through their evaluation and analysis.

The private caucus conversations are confidential. The exception occurs when the attorney for a disputant wishes that a certain fact or concept be expressly transmitted to the other side. Even though the caucus conversations are protected as confidential, the mediator will often encourage the parties to speak privately with their attorney, while stepping out of the room for a few minutes. The mediator does not desire to create a perception that she is dishonoring the attorney/client relationship and the communication that is involved within it. Further, the parties need to understand that the mediator respects them and that it is the mediator's hope that as the conversations continue through the day, the role of mediation and of the mediator will also be respected.

13.8 Negotiation Models and Objectives

A mediator may speculate on the question, "Is this party employing a negotiation model of some sort?" It can be fun and challenging to encounter such things. A mediator needs to be sufficiently flexible to accommodate any model that may be in play and open minded enough to enable the parties to change their model for negotiating purposes.

After sufficient substantive conversation has occurred regarding the basis for the dispute, the opportunity for opening negotiation arrives. This is a time to focus upon various methods of damage calculation. The plaintiff is usually well prepared to blackboard the categories for medical expenses, future medical expenses, loss of earning capacity, lost earnings, loss of consortium, pain and suffering, loss of the enjoyment of life, and other elements peculiar to the jurisdiction. Sometimes, verdicts in similar cases are vague yardsticks. Many settlements are confidential and therefore may not be usable, but experienced lawyers certainly know of those with which they had some participation or have a general sense for how various types of cases seem to be resolving. The insurance carriers know what they are paying for in various types of cases.

Such blackboard evaluations sometimes transition to some form of needs assessment. If the plaintiff has shared the opinion of a forensic economist regarding the loss of future earning capacity or the present value of a life care plan, this information can become an important foundation for crafting a meaningful portion of a resolution. If defense side opinions on such things have been shared, the relative cost analysis can be very helpful. It is common for both sides of the dispute to bring their own structure analysts, who have likely addressed the means of income replacement or future medical cost planning.

Disputes about money are not always about money. In the right case, an apology, written or oral, can be a very important and valuable contribution to the resolution of the dispute. Memorials, such as a planted tree, a piece of artwork, or a piece of sculpture, can be powerful contributions towards resolution. Only the imagination limits how such non-monetary aspects might be considered.

Sometimes, in the midst of a negotiation stream, the negotiation can be affected by the injection of some new information. Such information exchanges can be helpful in avoiding impasse or accelerating the discussion. However, if something is significantly material to the analysis and evaluation, it is probably far better to have shared it before the mediation than to introduce it during the mediation. If something is so significant and material, sometimes the better thing to do is suspend discussions and plan to resume them on another date.

13.9 Documenting the Deal

It is important that the parties have a memorandum of settlement in hand when they leave the mediation. While this practice may vary from state to state, the requirement in most is that the settlement be confirmed in writing. The mediator should encourage the parties to prepare the memorandum. The mediator can assist. Occasionally, there are unusual provisions that must be given strict attention to detail at that time, so as not to create differences when the formal release and settlement agreement appear later. The mediator should have an interest in assisting the parties in accomplishing an enduring settlement agreement.

13.10 Ethical Issues

The American Bar Association Model Rules of Professional Conduct, as adopted by various states, include discussion, rules, and commentary about lawyers as counselors, intermediaries, and dispute resolution neutrals. Various states have adopted additional ADR rules, which have incorporated standards of conduct for mediators.

13.11 Summary

The best mediations occur when the parties know more about the dispute, rather than less. Early mediations are good, in that the parties have the opportunity to avoid the cost, frustration, stress, anxiety, and systemic risk associated with the long path of litigation. However, such things and circumstances can perfectly illustrate the need for resolution, after the litigation has ripened and trial is just around the corner. The use and value of mediation will continue to evolve. That is a good thing.

Chapter 14

Structured Settlements

Frank Slesnick, Ph.D.

14.1 Introduction

This chapter will cover the topic of structured settlements. The introduction will give a brief description of structured settlements. The next section will describe the advantages and disadvantages of structured settlements from both the plaintiff's and defense perspectives. The following section examines the kinds of cases and phase of the case where such settlements typically arise. Following will be two sections that focus on the role of the economist. As will be explained, this role varies significantly based upon whether the economist is hired by the plaintiff or defense side. The last section provides some concluding comments.

As explained in earlier chapters, the common method of providing compensation in court cases is what is known as the lump-sum award. But for a variety of reasons (spelled out below), some participants in the legal process believe that it would be better if funds were distributed over time rather than as an immediate distribution. This is the basis of structured settlements.

Structured settlements are usually based upon annuity contracts issued by life insurance companies. Such contracts utilized within a court setting are what are known as "immediate annuity contracts" where the purchaser pays for the annuity in one payment. One of the nice features of these contracts is that there are a wide variety of disbursement patterns that can be specified. For example, the contract may provide a sum of money in the first period with increases at a fixed rate over time. It is also possible to specify lump-sum amounts such as the beginning period and fixed periods in subsequent years. Annuity contracts can pay out for a fixed period of time, for the life expectancy of the annuitant, or some combination of the two. For example, if John Smith has won a court award due to a catastrophic automobile accident, the future medical costs could be funded by an annuity contract that would provide funding for as long as Smith was alive or for twenty years, whichever was for the longest period.

If one or both of the parties in a lawsuit wish to propose a structured settlement, an annuitant is hired who will obtain bids from different life insurance companies. The quotes can vary substantially. The quote from a particular insurance company will depend upon the return the company expects to earn on its investments, its cost and profit structure, and the assumed life expectancy of the annuitant. Company A may believe that Smith will live a normal life expectancy of forty years while Company B believes Smith will live only twenty years. That factor will allow Company B to offer a lower premium for funding the contract. It is obvious that the insurance company must be financially reliable since Mr. Smith will be depending upon these funds, perhaps for the rest of his life. Further, the contract must conform to IRS guidelines in order for the contract to qualify for perhaps its biggest advantage over a lump-sum award—namely, its tax-free status. Specifically, although a lump-sum award is tax-free, the return from investing such an award generally is not. We shall now discuss the advantages and disadvantages of structured settlements and the role of an economist when they are proposed in court. We will focus on cases where the settlement is designed to fund future medical costs.

14.2 Advantages and Disadvantages

Perhaps the basic reason why structured settlements are used (aside from the fact that in some circumstances they are mandated by the court) is that they are mutually beneficial to both parties. Assume that the plaintiff's economist has estimated that Smith should receive $50,000 in the first year of loss and that this amount will increase 3 percent every year for the next thirty years. Payments are to fund future medical costs, a common reason for establishing a structured settlement. If the economist used a discount rate of 5 percent, the present value equal to the recommended lump-sum award would be $1,128,844. For convenience, the example will ignore the attorney's fee. What is important is that this sum of money is supposed to fund the future estimated losses. But what if the defense proposed a structured settlement that would provide the plaintiff $50,000 in the first period and that amount would increase 3 percent for the next thirty years, which is exactly equal to the estimated losses? At one level, the plaintiff should be indifferent between receiving the lump sum of $1,128,844 or a structured settlement that guaranteed the payouts indicated above. What is critical here is that an annuity contract can likely be purchased for well less than $1,128,844 from a life insurance company. The main reason why the company can do that is because it will ordinarily invest in securities that provide a return greater than the discount rate assumed by the plaintiff's economist (5 percent in our example).

Further, the company in many cases will assume the plaintiff will live a shorter time period than specified in the economist's calculations. Thus, the basic reason why structured settlements are often utilized is the fundamental idea that both the defense and the plaintiff's side are better off compared to providing funds through a lump-sum award. (See Chapter 14 on the CD for a detailed example.)

There are other reasons why Smith may find a structured settlement advantageous. If set up properly, payments received from the annuity contract are tax free. In contrast, interest earned from investing a lump-sum award is normally taxable unless the individual invests specifically in tax-free securities. Thus, in the example above, even if an amount equal to $1,128,844 earned 5 percent as predicted, the amount earned in the first year would not be $56,442 (1,128,844 * 0.05 = 56,442) but an amount less than that based upon the tax rate the plaintiff would have to pay. Second, if the contract is funding future medical costs, Smith may be uncertain whether he will outlive the thirty years assumed by the economist. The annuity contract can be written so that payments will continue for as long as he lives. Insurance companies can do this because they write many such contracts for individuals similar to Smith. Third, a contract will relieve Smith (or his family) of the burden of monitoring the portfolio over time. In a worst-case scenario, the family may actually utilize a lump-sum award for personal gain rather than for the benefit of Smith. A structured settlement will prevent that from happening. Fourth, a structured settlement will help avoid a rapid dissipation of the settlement, either by the plaintiff herself or individuals who can influence this decision. Finally, a structured settlement may reduce some of the conflict that naturally arises in legal cases. In particular, one area of contention may be Smith's life expectancy. As indicated above, an annuity contract can be written so that payments are made irrespective of how long Smith lives. The life expectancy issue has been taken off the table.

There are, however, several disadvantages if Smith agrees to a structured settlement. Perhaps the most important is that once a contract is written it cannot be altered in any way. Thus, if required costs rise by more than 3 percent (using the figure from our example), then Smith or his family cannot alter the rate of payout. A similar problem arises if there are unexpected emergencies such as unanticipated surgery. It is true that a lump-sum award cannot be altered, but such an award can be spent at a rate deemed appropriate by Smith. Further, Smith can alter his investment portfolio if the economic climate changes. For example, if interest rates rise rapidly, a flexible portfolio can take advantage of these higher returns. Second, it is possible that the insurance company could default on the payments. This problem can be avoided to some extent by carefully examining the financial viability of the insurance company. Third, the purpose of the settlement is to guarantee future funding of needed expenses. But there are many companies willing to buy the rights to a structured settlement. The amount received will be significantly lower than the present value of these payments calculated by the economist. Thus, one of the main arguments for structured settlements is undercut given the ability to sell the proceeds from the contract in the open market. Fourth, some have claimed that the plaintiff can always take the proceeds from a lump-sum award and buy an annuity, although there will be diminished tax advantages. Finally, there are a variety of philosophical arguments that focus on the fact that a structured settlement denies an individual, often severely injured, the right to spend money the way she sees fit. There may, of course, be ways for getting around some of these problems. For example, the problem of costs rising faster than anticipated can be partially solved by increasing payments at a rate somewhat faster than forecast. Periodic lump-sum awards may handle the problem of medical emergencies. Or a "Special Needs Trust" can be established where funds are available to the plaintiff but only if deemed necessary.

Before leaving this discussion, it must be noted that, in general, the plaintiff's attorneys have been more averse to utilizing structured settlements than the defense side. A reason is that the attorney's fee is based upon the lower cost of the annuity rather than the present value of future medical costs as calculated by the plaintiff's economist (assuming that the jury has awarded a similar amount).

14.3 When Structured Settlements Are Used

A typical case where a structured settlement is appropriate is a catastrophic injury that requires significant future medical costs. Related, it may be appropriate when there is significant uncertainty concerning life expectancy. Another common factor is the age of the plaintiff. If the individual is a minor, there may be concern that the guardians will not adequately insure that funds are available for the child's medical needs. Others have suggested the following types of cases: a death case where minor children must be cared for; cases where the interest earned on a lump-sum award will subject the individual to a high tax rate; or cases where the plaintiff may need protection to preserve the award.

The proposal of a structured settlement typically occurs prior to trial. However, there is no reason why the defense could not offer such a settlement during the trial or even after the jury has made its decision. In fact, in some jurisdictions it is necessary that payments for some cases be in the form of a structured settlement.

14.4 The Role of the Economist Evaluating Structured Settlements—The Defense Perspective

As indicated above, structured settlements almost always arise as a proposal from the defense side. Further, an annuitist is required to obtain bids from insurance companies. What, then, is the role of the economist hired by the defense? The annuitist will use future medical costs as estimated by the economist. These projections must be in nominal rather than real terms (adjusted for inflation) since that is a requirement for pricing an annuity. It may be the figures projected by the plaintiff's economist, but there is no reason why the economist hired by the defense could not independently calculate future medical costs. This separate calculation will differ from the estimates of the plaintiff's economist for a number of reasons. An obvious reason is that the defense economist is utilizing a life care plan developed specifically by a life care planner hired by the defense. Second, the defense economist may have different assumptions concerning the rate of increase in medical costs. Third, life expectancy assumptions may differ, although this point is normally irrelevant given payments are made for the life of the plaintiff. The defense economist may also be asked to explain why a structured settlement is a reasonable way to fund future medical costs in contrast to providing the plaintiff a lump-sum award. That is, the economist will go through the pros and the cons of structured settlements.

14.5 The Role of the Economist Evaluating Structured Settlements—The Plaintiff's Perspective

The plaintiff's economist's report may have served as the basis for projecting medical costs utilized by the annuitist. The proposed structured settlement then covers those costs that the plaintiff's side has, in fact, stated will occur. It is important to note, however, that the annuitist will use nominal growth rates when pricing a structured settlement. This can cause difficulties if the economist's report adjusted future medical costs for the rate of inflation. If the plaintiff's economist knows that her report might be used to price a structured settlement, she may project future medical costs using nominal rather than real growth rates. In addition, the plaintiff's economist may be asked to calculate the cost of the annuity since normally this is not freely divulged. This may be important if the plaintiff attorney's fee is based on this figure. There are two pieces of information about which the economist is uncertain. First, he does not know what discount rate the insurance company utilized to discount future payouts. However, if the economist is reasonably conversant with how insurance companies operate, he may be able to make a fairly precise estimate. What the economist cannot know is, what life expectancy did the insurance company assume? The lower the assumed life expectancy, the lower the cost of the annuity.

The plaintiff's economist may also be asked to calculate the present value of an annuity that does not necessarily follow the estimated medical costs as outlined in a life care plan. Perhaps the proposed settlement has added certain lump-sum values to be paid out at various time periods. Or the settlement incorporates a different rate of increase in medical costs. These future costs can be discounted either at the discount rate used by the economist in her report or at the estimated discount rate used by the insurance company. The former can be used to compare the present value of the proposal with the present value as estimated by the economist in her trial report. It is doubtful that a proposal that is significantly less than the original present value would be acceptable.

14.6 Concluding Comments

Structured settlements are becoming more widespread as a way of funding future medical costs and periodic lump-sum payments. Although less common, they may also be used to fund future lost earnings. The basic reason why such settlements are used is that for certain types of cases and if properly set up, they can benefit both sides of the case. An economist can assist the attorney in a variety of ways. The defense economist can estimate future medical costs for a life care plan proposed by the defense. She can also discuss in general terms how an annuity contrasts with lump-sum awards and what are the advantages and disadvantages of each approach. The plaintiff's economist can be used to estimate the cost of the annuity to the insurance company and determine the present value of a structured settlement proposal that incorporates a different pattern of future medical costs than originally estimated. In addition, he can explain the difference between funding through a structured settlement and a lump-sum award, but perhaps with a different perspective than the defense economist in terms of which approach is best for the plaintiff. The CD for Chapter 14 will provide a simple example showing how a structured settlement can benefit both the plaintiff and the defense. In addition, some references are listed which relate to the material in this chapter.

Chapter 15

The Plaintiff Attorney's Perspective on Economic Damages at Trial

R. Edison Hill, Esq.

The gathering of thoughts concerning economic damages and proof thereof should begin with the initial interview of a potential client. For purposes of this discussion, economic damages on behalf of the plaintiff will be limited to personal injury cases and wrongful death cases. In most jurisdictions, economic damages must be proven by a preponderance of the evidence; and, therefore, the more concrete and objective your evidence of economic damages, the greater the persuasive value of such evidence.

15.1 Types of Economic Damages in Personal Injury Cases

A. Medical costs—past and future

Past medical expenses are easy to document, but it is necessary to ensure all past medical expenses have been acquired. Documentation by way of invoices for hospital expenses and those of treating physicians, therapists, and any other medical care expenses should be obtained. Do not forget that all prescription medications and over-the-counter medications are included as past medical expenses, so long as a testifying medical provider or expert says that such medications were reasonable and necessary to treat the injuries or relieve pain for injuries sustained. Identities of all healthcare providers should be obtained in the initial client interview and updated as your client continues treatment with healthcare professionals. For use of medical bills and records throughout the litigation and for trial purposes, you may want to Bates stamp these documents and have them authenticated for evidentiary purposes through use of requests for admissions under the applicable rules of civil procedure.

As for future medical expenses, this information may come from treating healthcare providers or a non-treating healthcare provider expert, hired for the purpose of providing cohesive testimony regarding future healthcare needs. A life care planner, as an expert witness, can also provide very valuable admissible evidence regarding future healthcare costs. The life care planner is especially useful where injuries are permanent and require long-term or lifetime medical interventions. Normally, the life care planner consults with each medical care provider to acquire the pertinent information regarding the type of examinations, treatment, surgery, therapy, or medications that are necessary for future care, based upon a reasonable degree of medical probability. The life care planner also obtains frequency of such medical needs and the costs of the same at current-day prices and at costs pertinent for the applicable locality. A forensic economist will then attach the appropriate inflation rates to the various categories of medical, care, and related costs and discount future values to a present value loss at trial.

B. Loss of income—past and future

If your injured client has lost income as a result of her injuries, document those losses to the extent possible. Income tax returns generally are the best source to show loss of income. Compare past tax returns to tax returns showing less income following an injury due to the inability to work because of injuries. Social Security earnings statements, W-2 forms, payroll records, and pay stubs depicting differences in earnings before and after sustaining injuries are other sources for documenting lost income. It will be necessary to demonstrate that work was available to your injured client, and that she was unable to work and thereby earn income solely because of the injuries at issue.

If your client earned income but did not report it to the taxing authorities, that raises other obvious legal implications. You do not want to expose your client to criminal sanctions and/or substantial civil penalties for failure to report income. If you find yourself in this dilemma, first check to see if your client's income rose to the level of legally required reporting. If not, and if you can document lost income below the reporting level, then you are justified in doing so.

On the other hand, if your client earned income over the annual level requiring reporting, then you have the choice of either not claiming loss of income, thereby protecting your client from criminal sanctions or civil penalties, or you can seek to file late income tax returns and let your client pay any overdue income tax and fines. In some situations, this may be a justifiable position to take on behalf of your client, and thereby pursue a claim for loss of past or future income.

If your injured client was gainfully employed both before and after sustaining injury, you may still have a claim for diminished earning capacity. Assuming that your client's injury would affect his employability if for any reason the current employment should be lost, then you should explore this avenue of damages. Typically, you will hire a vocational rehabilitation expert to help with this evaluation. This expert should examine all medical records and read all medical reports. The vocational rehabilitation expert should examine all restrictions placed by treating physicians on your client and test your injured client for aptitude for jobs that can be performed with the limitations placed by his healthcare providers. This expert should then perform a job market survey to determine the availability and pay for jobs that your client can perform with the injuries. You will need to make your client available for aptitude testing and an interview by your vocational rehabilitation expert. After having performed these tasks, this expert will generally prepare a detailed report of your client's pre-injury jobs and earnings and an evaluation of post-injury job possibilities, the likely earnings therefrom, and perhaps the reduction in a normal worklife expectancy.

In order to have the value of your diminished income-earning capacity in a form ready to be introduced as evidence at trial, provide this report to your forensic economist. Your forensic economist will make the necessary and appropriate computations for your injured client, for her worklife expectancy, and arrive at a present-day value of your injured client's diminished income-earning capacity. This may be expressed in the form of a range of expected monetary loss, rather than an exact amount. A range of loss in this regard may be more credible to a jury than a loss expressed in one exact monetary amount.

C. Loss of household services

Do not overlook the value of loss of household services, if allowed in your jurisdiction. For household services that your client was unable to perform from the date of injury to the date of trial, your client may have had to pay someone to perform services that he would have performed had the injuries not been sustained. Those past services that have been purchased are obvious damages for which your client can recover. On the other hand, if family members or friends have gratuitously provided household services that would otherwise have been provided by your injured client, then check your jurisdiction to see if a value can be placed upon gratuitous household services performed. In all likelihood, by detailing the number of hours per week of such household service performed and the type of actual service performed, you can recover for an acceptable hourly rate of pay. Most qualified housecleaning services charge more than minimum wage, so you probably will not be limited to seeking only a minimum wage payment for gratuitous loss of household services.

For future loss of household services and to calculate a present-day value for this often overlooked element of damages, you must provide your forensic economist with a detailed list of household services provided during a typical week or month, setting forth the time that your injured client, before injury, spent performing such household services. Compare that with those household services your injured client can no longer perform. Through your medical evidence, ascertain if these projected losses of future household services are permanent, or the inability to perform certain household services is for a limited period of time (usually expressed in a range of time). Armed with this information, your forensic economist will be able to calculate the present-day value of future loss of household services. If the loss of household services is for a lifetime, then your forensic economist will utilize life expectancy tables to determine the appropriate number of years for making such a calculation.

Before trial, ensure you have updated responses to defense discovery requests, so as to reflect loss of household services. Keep this item of damages in mind in preparing your client for a discovery deposition, as you want to make sure that not only written discovery responses are consistent with your client's claim for future loss of household services, but that your client's own testimony in her discovery deposition is consistent as well.

In examining loss of household services, be careful to review with your client his chores and repair activities at home. Although husbands usually spend more time away from the home than the wife, the husband is more likely to be involved in home job activities such as cutting the grass, making household repairs, managing finances, moving furniture, shoveling snow, raking leaves, performing other lawn care activities, making investments, and handling finances for the family. The wife most often is responsible for cooking, taking care of children, washing clothes, cleaning the home, engaging in general housekeeping, transporting children, providing nursing activities to sick family members, and otherwise running household errands (although traditional roles are changing in two-earner families). All of these activities fall into the category of household services. It would be extremely difficult to find one person who could be hired to perform all of these services that can no longer be performed due to injury. Therefore, it is very important to make accurate estimates of time consumed for each activity that can be identified as being a valuable household service previously performed by your injured client. In calculating the value of lost household services, you may need to identify a range of costs that you have to pay to have such services performed. Your forensic economist will be able to help with appropriate government-provided data for this task.

When examining and evaluating lost household services, be sure to investigate unusual services that your injured client may have performed before being injured that have value and for which damages can be calculated and claimed. For instance, some men are handier around the house than others, in that they possess skills for certain household repairs that most people spend money to have performed. An injured husband may have particular carpentry skills and can repair things around the home that an average husband would need to pay to have done. Or, the same may be true for electrical or plumbing skills. An injured wife may have been an accomplished interior decorator, a maker of crafts or have the ability to make clothing for the family. In special cases such as these, it is appropriate to seek compensation for value of such services at a greater rate of pay than for more regular or mundane household services.

D. Hedonic damages (quantifying loss of enjoyment of life)

"Hedonic" or "hedonism" refers to life's pleasure or happiness. Some refer to hedonic values as that which is good or desirable in life. In the last twenty years or so, hedonic damages have developed as a separate and distinct loss that is measurable in serious personal injury cases and in some wrongful death cases. This item of damage is separate and distinct from economic loss of income or any other type of special damages. One reason it is distinctly different is because it is a "measurable" or economic damage, and it is not to be confused with general damages that are not directly measurable, such as pain and suffering, mental anguish, loss of consortium, or loss of companionship.

Before getting too excited about this form of damages, check the law in your jurisdiction. A number of states have expressly banned hedonic damages as an element of damages for which one can seek compensation. There is disagreement among economists as to the propriety of inclusion of hedonic damages as a form of compensable damages. A forensic economist is generally utilized to calculate hedonic damages based upon a variety of factors. The forensic economist does not measure the pleasures of life for a particular individual, but instead, values a statistically average person by utilizing a variety of economic studies, studies by human behavior experts, and government research. These studies are generally based on what workers or consumers are willing to pay to lower their risks of death or serious injury—in lower wages for safer jobs or for airbags or other safety products as examples. The forensic economist generally will not place a specific dollar value on life, but will provide a range of values to which a jury, if permitted, will apply its own collective judgment. The range of the dollar value placed on life is often a very large range, typically between $500,000 and $3.5 million, but some economists testify to much larger values. Some states allow testimony on such damages only in cases involving serious permanent injuries, while some states allow value of life testimony in wrongful death cases.

15.2 Types of Economic Damages in Wrongful Death Cases

A. Medical and funeral costs

In a wrongful death case, if your decedent has incurred medical bills from hospitalization, medical treatment, and/or emergency transportation (ambulance, aircraft, or emergency watercraft), acquire all medical and billing records regarding these expenses. Even in cases of traumatically induced death that occurs very quickly, without prolonged suffering or medical treatment, there are often extensive costs associated with emergency transportation and heroic medical efforts to revive the accident victim before death is pronounced. Most jurisdictions allow reasonable funeral and burial expenses as a part of the economic damages in wrongful death cases.

B. Loss of future earnings resulting from death

The obvious starting point here is to determine your decedent's level of income at the time of death. Income tax and Social Security Administration records, payroll records, W-2 forms, and pay stubs from employment are the primary sources for the documents necessary to establish the level of income at death. Identify all employer-paid benefits and the amount paid for each, such as for Social Security, health insurance premiums, life insurance premiums, disability insurance premiums, and pension plan contributions. Obtain income-earning records for a period of between five and ten years. If you cannot locate these records from your decedent's personal records or from her family members, ascertain whether or not your decedent utilized the services of an accounting firm and, if so, seek past income tax records from that source. If income tax records are not available from these sources, utilize Form 4506 from the Internal Revenue Service and apply for copies of past income tax returns. It takes several months (minimally two months) to acquire records from the Internal Revenue Service so make application early to avoid waiting for these necessary records before you can make appropriate income loss computations. If your decedent earned income but did not report it to the taxing authorities, this has legal implications that were previously discussed.

In gathering information for your forensic economist to analyze and evaluate loss of future income due to death, identify your decedent's level of education and occupational history. This information is critical in analyzing and determining your decedent's loss of income from the time of death until the likely time of retirement had he lived.

It is also critical to gather information from a variety of sources concerning your decedent's state of health at the time of death. While you want to gather as much information as possible from a surviving spouse and close family members, it is highly recommended that you seek medical records from your decedent's primary care physician for the last five to ten years. The more you can utilize medical records to show that your decedent was in good health at the time of death, the less your economic analysis for future loss of income will be subject to attack on cross-examination. If your decedent did suffer from one or more diseases, you need to show to the extent possible that such disease was stabilized and was being medically managed. For instance, if your decedent had a history of heart attack, you hope to show from medical records that she recovered from that heart attack and followed medical advice by maintaining appropriate weight and perhaps taking cholesterol-reducing medication on a regular basis. You are then more likely to survive attempts by opposing counsel to attack the credibility of your economist's analysis of loss of future income. On the other hand, the defense will attempt to show that your decedent's health would have likely precluded her from maintaining gainful employment until attaining retirement age.

C. Personal consumption

In most jurisdictions, for wrongful death cases, a deduction must be made for the amount of income that would have been consumed personally by the decedent. Check the law in your jurisdiction on this subject. A few states do not allow a deduction for personal consumption in wrongful death cases, which makes a substantial difference in the amount of economic damages one can present at trial.

Since as a practical matter no one keeps a record of the amount of family income used for each family member, the measurement of this adjustment, or deduction for personal consumption, can be a difficult but not impossible issue to address. Forensic economists specialize in the measurement of personal consumption or minimum "maintenance" spending, and this topic has been covered in Chapter 8.

15.3 Presenting Economic Damages at Trial
A. Voir dire and damages

Plant the seeds of your damages in voir dire. In some jurisdictions, voir dire questions must be submitted to the judge for approval. If given a choice, it is better to ask voir dire questions yourself, rather than having the judge ask them. While you might talk the judge into asking follow-up questions, the judge will not know the case nearly as well as you, and you will be more sensitive to asking follow-up questions of jurors requiring more than a "yes" or "no" answer. These questions flush out those jurors who have a bias and whom you may want to challenge for cause, or in the alternative, eliminate with a preemptory strike.

It is recommended that your jury voir dire questions be short and open-ended. "How do you feel about . . ." or "Please tell me about . . ." instead of "Do you . . ." type questions. Listen to your jurors' responses and watch their reactions. By doing so, you will be more sensitive to the types of follow-up voir dire questions to ask. Open-ended questions cannot be answered by "yes" or "no"; but rather require thought and a responsive phrase, sentence, or more. Remember, your goal is both to gather information and responses from your voir dire and to provide information to your jurors about your case.

A closed-ended question might be utilized for the limited purpose of introducing a new subject matter series of questions. An example is "How many of you are familiar with life expectancy tables? Please raise your hands." Then, depending on their responses, you can ask a series of open-ended questions. The most important aspect of voir dire is the follow-up questions that require jurors to respond. In response to "How many of you have been in a car wreck?", you will probably have several affirmative responses. Go to each juror who responded affirmatively and ask the following open-ended question (or something similar): "What can you tell me about it?" Then, depending on their response, you may have other open-ended questions, such as questions about injuries sustained, for that particular juror.

Make sure in voir dire that you convey the concept of the burden of proof in a civil case: your burden is to show "by a preponderance of the evidence," unlike a criminal trial which requires a burden of proof "beyond all reasonable doubt." Ensure jurors know that this lower burden of proof applies to evidence about damages. You want the jury to realize early on that there is some room for doubt in a civil case, including evidence pertaining to damages, and yet, the plaintiff can still meet his burden of proof.

If you have been provided adequate time to conduct proper voir dire of your jury, you will have laid a valuable foundation for your jurors to receive your evidence of damages and appreciate that all you are attempting to do is give jurors an opportunity to "make whole" your injured client or family members who have lost a loved one. This also will set the stage for your opening statement.

B. Opening statement regarding economic damages

While it is doubtful that jurors ever decide a case after opening statements, by the end of voir dire and the opening statements, jurors have developed certain unalterable beliefs as to what the case is about. These beliefs govern much of how they weigh the evidence presented during trial and what they will ultimately decide during jury deliberations.

In preparing your opening statement, remember that we are in an era of "tort reform." When you, as a plaintiff lawyer, stand in front of a jury at the beginning of trial, you have virtually no credibility. You cannot ask the jury to believe you about anything, and you cannot expect the jury to accept your conclusory remarks ("As a result of his injuries, John Smith will lose over $1 million of income in the future."). As the plaintiff lawyer, you will have to earn your credibility as you proceed during the trial. Let the jury know early on that your trial is about harm and about damages. If you place too much emphasis on liability, the jury will focus more on liability and less on damages, possibly resulting in a verdict for the plaintiff, but with low damages. Let the jury know early in your opening statement that this trial is about what will be required to make up for the harm caused to your client. You want the jury to bear this in mind throughout the trial, even if your first witnesses have to do with liability and not damages.

Credibility is everything. Every action on your part as plaintiff's attorney: every word you say, every movement you make, and your appearance from head to toe, bears upon your credibility. Do not waste words and do not waste time. Jurors will consider it disrespectful towards them if you waste their time and if you are not prepared. Go slowly, but steadily. You want to give jurors time to absorb every point you attempt to make. If you are a rapid speaker, jurors will miss something, and it might be very important. Do not ask or expect the jury to take your word for anything. They won't. If you do not back up every representation you make in opening statement with a fact witness, an expert, a photograph, or some bit of evidence, it will bear adversely upon your credibility, and likewise upon the ultimate outcome.

Remember to talk like a normal person and avoid at all costs talking like someone who went to law school. Use plain English and do not put on pretenses or try to be someone that you are not. If you come across as being "fake," your credibility will suffer. Dress approachably. Avoid flashy dress and jewelry. Avoid a "slick" look because this is the stereotypical "slick trial lawyer" that jurors have been brainwashed into believing about you before your trial begins.

Eye contact is more valuable than you can imagine. While you should avoid staring at jurors, make eye contact with every juror during your opening statement. Genuine eye contact promotes credibility. Avoid prancing back and forth as you speak to the jury in opening statement. Stand generally in one place and talk to the jurors. Move if you have reason to do so, but walking around as you speak to the jury suggests nervousness and undermines your credibility. It is recommended that you rehearse your opening statement several times. Videotaping yourself so you can watch it is a better idea than rehearsing in front of a mirror.

Avoid memorizing your opening statement to the jury. It will sound fake and memorized. Above all, do not read your opening statement. At most, use a one-page outline that you can glance at and then concentrate on making eye contact as you speak to the jury.

In discussing damages, let the jury know of the losses and harms to your client. Depending on the nature of your case, it is suggested that one-third to one-half of your opening statement deal with damages. When you begin talking about the damages, try not to slip back into the topic of negligence or fault. Jurors want to deal with one issue at a time. Explain in your opening statement why you need to show the losses and harms and that the reason for doing so has nothing to do with sympathy. This trial is not about sympathy. It is about how much money it will take to make up for your client's losses and harms. Let the jury know this must be the basis of their decision on the amount of damages.

In order to set the stage for discussing loss of income, past and future, you must identify the tasks of life and work that your client can no longer do or cannot do to the extent that she previously did as a result of injuries sustained. In a wrongful death case, explain to the jury what has happened to the family since Dad, the family's breadwinner, was killed. Do not generalize as you make these points, but, rather, use a handful of specific examples. Make sure you provide evidence later in your case to back up each example.

If you plan to introduce evidence of a life care plan, you may want to consider referring to it as a "minimum life care plan," so as to convey the message that this is the amount of money that will have to be awarded in order to provide the minimum humane level of care, comfort, and safety for your injured client. Since life care plans are based upon life expectancy, explain in your opening statement that your minimum life care planner will testify that many people the same age as your injured client will live longer than this age that has been pulled from a government life expectancy table. This not only reinforces the "minimum" argument, but it also counters any defense argument that the permanent disability lowers life expectancy and, thereby, the period of needed care.

Some jurisdictions allow the plaintiff's lawyer to identify in opening statement the monetary amount desired in the final verdict. If your jurisdiction allows it, do it. Jurors want to be told the amount needed to make the plaintiff whole. On the other hand, many jurisdictions do not permit the plaintiff's attorney to ask for a total amount desired in a verdict, but even in those jurisdictions, it is permissible to review the amounts of the various economic damages. Again, it is advisable to do so and to get these figures out to the jury in opening statement. You want the jury to be thinking about these amounts as they hear what the defendant did wrong that caused this harm and loss to your client.

C. Closing argument regarding economic damages

Closing argument is the culmination of all that has previously transpired in a trial. The plaintiff's lawyer is generally considered to have an advantage in closing argument by being permitted the opportunity to both begin the closing argument aspect of trial and also to end this last portion of the trial.

It is critical that you understand and follow the rules covering closing argument in your jurisdiction. Most courts establish a time limit on closing argument, and some will literally cut you off in mid-sentence when you have reached your limit. If permitted, ask beforehand for the number of minutes permitted for closing argument and request more time than you actually expect to use. Time flies by in this last and critical stage of the trial as you are reviewing the evidence, including all aspects of damages. It is better to have more time than you need than to find yourself running out of time and unable to cover the various subjects desired in closing argument. Most jurisdictions require a "fair opening." This means that you cannot hold in reserve for your ending close (after the defense has made closing argument) topics or evidence that you have not covered in the opening or beginning part of your closing argument. The ending portion of the plaintiff's closing argument is normally restricted to replying or responding to the defense argument; and counsel for plaintiff is normally prohibited from raising new subjects in the final portion of closing argument.

Commonly, at least one-half of the time allotted for plaintiff's closing argument is attributed to the opening portion of closing argument. Therefore, since counsel for plaintiff has the opportunity to have the last say by providing a reply closing argument, no more than one-half of the allotted time may be utilized for the ending portion of closing argument. This rule prohibits plaintiff's counsel from saving most of the closing argument time to respond to the defense argument, and thereby gain unfair advantage.

Assuming liability is a contested issue at trial, it is wise to spend at least half of your closing argument time in discussing damages. Failure to do this risks an award of money that is lower than expected. If discussing the amount to award is worthy of considerable jury deliberation (which is most desirable), then it is worth sending the right message to the jury in closing argument by spending an appropriate amount of time on it. If you spend 80 percent of your closing argument time on liability and 20 percent on damages, the likelihood of the jury awarding an inadequate amount of monetary damages is substantial.

Visual presentation enhances jury appreciation of evidence. You may want to consider seeking court permission to allow jurors to take notes during closing argument (and perhaps throughout the trial if you think that is appropriate and your jurisdiction allows it). Or, at the very least, it is recommended that all elements of your damages be visually displayed before the jury during closing argument and that each element be discussed and the supporting evidence reviewed. However, beware of just rehashing the evidence. Jurors are likely to consider "rehashing" to be a waste of their time.

If your rules permit, have a copy of the court-approved verdict form for your case and visually present it to the jury during closing argument. If your jurisdiction permits the itemizing of each element of compensatory damages on the verdict form, do not pass up the opportunity to have a blank space for each element of damages on the verdict form and a space for a total at the bottom. Itemized economic damages include, but are not limited to, past medical costs, present-day value of future medical costs (present-day value of the life care plan), past loss of income, present-day value of future loss of income (and/or present-day value of diminished income capacity), loss of household services, funeral costs, and hedonic damages (for jurisdictions permitting it). When jurors are required to think through and discuss each item of damage permitted in your case, most likely the total award will be greater than if jurors are simply allowed to award a lump sum for compensatory damages. Based on the evidence you have presented, describe to the jury the amount of money that should be placed in each blank on the jury verdict form. You may demonstrate this in a variety of ways, but one simple method in which to present this visually to a jury is to utilize a large paper flip board on an easel, using broad felt-tipped colored markers to write figures large and distinctly in the blanks, based upon evidence presented. So long as the amounts you are asking the jury to fill in the blank spaces on the verdict form are fair, just, and supported by the evidence, and you no more than make your plaintiff whole financially, jurors welcome the opportunity for you to tell them what they need to do. Don't miss this opportunity.

It is recommended that you spend some time towards the end of your closing argument empowering the jurors by letting them know the importance of their actions. They need to leave the courtroom and begin deliberations with your words ringing in their ears that "only you have the power and the authority to right this wrong, the wrong committed by the defendant that created a debt by the defendant to the plaintiff." Jurors need to know that this is the one and only opportunity that the plaintiff has to seek redress for the harm caused by the defendant.

During closing argument, discuss the most important jury instructions. Research tells us that jurors do not understand what they are being read in the form of jury instructions. They may remember a word or a phrase, but it is often taken out of context. Take the most important instructions bearing upon damages and explain those instructions and the terminology in very simple language. Use illustrations to make your point. For instance, jury instructions that deal with compensating the plaintiff are often misunderstood. Explain that compensation or "to compensate" requires the jury to take affirmative action—to do something. To compensate means to balance the harm on one side with an award of money on the other side.

If your jurisdiction has comparative fault or negligence, and that is an issue in your case, make sure you explain the effect of negligence attributed to the plaintiff upon the award of damages. In many jurisdictions, the jury is not to reduce for negligence on the part of the plaintiff, but rather the court does that after the verdict is in. If this is not explained and understood by jurors, the effect could be a doubling of diminution of damages for negligence on the part of the plaintiff, if both jurors and the court subtract for negligence of the plaintiff.

Although you may have discussed the burden of proof in the civil cases during opening statement, it is critical that the jury begin deliberations with the understanding that the burden of proof in a civil case simply means "more likely than not." A simple method of demonstrating this is to use your hands to simulate scales of justice while explaining to the jury that if all of the evidence received on one side of the scales ever so slightly outweighs the evidence on the other side of the scales, then on that particular issue, the jury may find in favor of the plaintiff. You may want to contrast this with the burden of proof in a criminal case, in which "proof beyond a reasonable doubt" requires the scales to be tipped far down in favor of the prosecuting agency in order for a jury to convict a person accused of committing a crime. Remember, jurors do not understand "burden of proof," but they do understand "more probable than not." You can use this approach in discussing each item of damages.

This chapter has largely been devoted to economic damages at trial. However, during closing argument, the total amount of economic damages awarded by a jury can and should be used as a springboard to argue the non-economic damages, such as pain and suffering and loss of enjoyment of life (if your jurisdiction does not permit hedonic damages). You may want to argue that value of the non-economic losses or intangible losses far outweighs the economic damages and should be a multiple of the total amount of economic damages, considering the severity of the injuries, the permanency of the injuries, the devastating effect of the injuries upon the plaintiff, and so forth. If your jurisdiction permits you to argue a sum certain for non-economic damages, then by all means do so. Again, jurors appreciate and want to be told what they need to do to make a fair and just award of money to the plaintiff. However, if permitted to make such argument, you may want to speak in the form of a range of an award of money, especially as it relates to non-economic damages.

Make it clear in your closing argument that you do not want sympathy from the jurors. All you want and expect them to do is to make a fair and just award of money in order to balance the scales, providing money for the harm caused by the defendant. Research indicates that by the time closing argument begins during the trial, most jurors have made up their minds to a great degree. What you endeavor to accomplish most during closing argument is to arm those jurors who are your advocates with ammunition to persuade those jurors who are against you. To supply these juror advocates with evidence and reasoning to argue during deliberation on your behalf will greatly enhance the likelihood of a jury verdict that is fair and just to the plaintiff.

Chapter 16

A Defense Trial Lawyer on Damage Issues at Deposition and Trial

E. Wayne Taff, Esq.

16.1 Introduction

Other chapters in this book have addressed specific economic issues relating to a variety of precise topics—how an economist calculates projected wage loss, fringe benefits, and a host of other specific types of damages. While this chapter will re-examine some of those topics, it will do so from a different perspective—that of the defense trial lawyer, addressing what the defense lawyer does to prepare to persuade the audience that counts: the jury.

In analyzing how the defense trial lawyer accomplishes his task, it is important to distinguish the role of the plaintiff's lawyer/plaintiff's economist from the role of the defense lawyer/defense economist. While it is self-evident that the role of the plaintiff is to maximize damages and the role of the defense is to defeat or minimize the damage claim, what is not self-evident is that frequently the goal of minimization is not achieved through a defense economist, but instead by turning the plaintiff's economist into a defense witness. Similarly, it is not self-evident that at every step, at every question in deposition, at every question on cross-examination and every question on direct examination, the defense lawyer must always ask one question of herself: does this help achieve the goal of defeat or minimization? If not, the action should not be taken, nor the question asked.

A final introductory note: This chapter primarily addresses personal injury or wrongful death cases. The views of the defense lawyer in commercial cases are saved for another day. Similarly, since it would take another entire book to treat punitive damages meaningfully, punitive damages are not treated in depth.

16.2 Success Begins Long Before Trial: The "Discovery" Process

As in most endeavors in life, trial success is achieved by preparation, preparation, and more preparation. In the trial context, in most jurisdictions, preparation is accomplished through written discovery and depositions of expert witnesses. Now for two bits of advice about taking the deposition of the plaintiff's expert. First, while it is true that you may need to "discover" certain information during the deposition, the primary purpose of the deposition is to commit the expert to propositions that are favorable to your position. If you do not know what those propositions are or do not know how you are going to get the expert to agree with those propositions, you are not ready. Do not take the deposition! Second, the logical conclusion from the first tip: preparation for the deposition is critical and, indeed, likely far more critical than your preparation for the actual trial cross-examination.

16.3 When Do You Retain the Defense Economist?

At best, the defense economist should be retained before the discovery process begins, or, at worst, before substantive discovery takes place. As outlined below, certain information must be obtained in order to be prepared to examine plaintiff's economist. The defense economist is likely in the best position to advise the defense lawyer regarding the documents that should be discovered in order to properly examine plaintiff's economist and the materials that he will need to form well-grounded opinions. Similarly, early retention permits defense counsel to furnish the report from plaintiff's economist to the defense economist who, in turn, can provide advice to defense counsel regarding the assumptions made, the flaws in those assumptions or the data, and the questions that should be asked to demonstrate the weaknesses in the report from plaintiff's economist.

16.4 The "Data" You Need for Depositions

First, gather the necessary information through the written discovery process or through the deposition of the plaintiff. Get plaintiff to tell you about all of his past employments, about his job duties, and the earnings, amount and frequency of raises at those employments. Find out what work he claims he can no longer do and what work he claims he can do. Find out how much work he really performed at home before the accident and how many hours he spends doing that work. But don't stop there. Get the tax returns. Get the employment records—all of them. Get the union contract. Get the Social Security earnings records. Get the educational and vocational training records. Obtain the federal and state publications identifying the earnings by race, age, education, and employment category for your area of the country. Why get this data? Because if the plaintiff's economist has done her job, she has gotten it and relied—or purportedly relied—upon it for her opinions, and that data forms—or should form—the bases for the opinions. You, the lawyer, have to know what the data are to be able to know that the economist, in fact, ignored or overstated the data.

Get the expert's professional résumé. Does the expert belong to professional societies? Do those societies publish standards? Do those standards explain what it is the expert must have done to prepare his report? Did the expert do those things?

Obtain every published writing of the expert, including economic studies performed by the expert that were not prepared for litigation purposes. Do those writings contain favorable statements that will support your propositions? Obtain every prior deposition or trial transcript you can obtain. What do they say that is favorable to your case? Did the expert testify to a preferred methodology or data source in an earlier case and ignore it in this one? Did the expert fail to obtain in your case a detailed survey completed by the plaintiff that she earlier testified was a critical source of information for a proper evaluation? If the expert teaches, find out what courses she has taught and the textbooks she uses. Do those textbooks from which she teaches set forth economic propositions favorable to your case, totally disregarded by the very teacher who uses the book to teach would-be economists?

16.5 Structuring the Examination at Deposition

If you start the deposition by saying, "you would agree with me that your opinions are invalid because you considered plaintiff's earnings for only one year, rather than five," I guarantee you will not get the answer you like. The moral of the story is simple: commit the expert to general propositions before ever asking case-specific questions. Ask questions with which the expert must agree or look foolish or extreme.

Examples: "You would agree with me an economist attempts to predict the future? You would agree with me that predicting the future is an inexact science? You would agree that you are not telling the jury what 'would have been?' Instead, you are telling the jury what 'might have been?' You agree with me that economic predictions are like all predictions—you have only a 50-50 chance of being right? I mean, after all, you are either right or you are wrong, and there is no way for this jury to know today whether your projection for something occurring fifteen years from now is a correct prediction, since you don't even know that yourself? You would agree that the accuracy of your prediction is entirely dependent on the assumptions you have made? In fact, if even one of those assumptions is wrong, then your prediction is wrong, correct? You agree with me that when making long-term projections of economic wage loss, one should, where possible, base that prediction on the earnings of the plaintiff over a long period of time before his accident?" And so on.

It is only after you have asked those questions and gotten the right answers that you ask the case-specific questions. And, even then, you have to decide whether you save those questions for trial, at the risk of asking them now and having plaintiff get a new economist. Do you ask now or later questions along the following line: "Sir, it's true, is it not, that you only considered plaintiff's wage for the year of the accident and the year before, although he had worked at the same employer for twenty years? And you know, don't you, that if you had considered his entire twenty-year employment, that he averaged a raise of only 1.2 percent per year, instead of the 15 percent you got by using his raise just before the accident? Ma'am, it's true, is it not, that you were told that plaintiff had not worked since the accident, and nobody told you that she had been working at XY but not reporting her income to the federal government?"

16.6 What Was Done and What Was Not Done by the Economist
While it is important to find out what the plaintiff's economist did, it is frequently far more important to find out what they did not do and why they did not do it. Did he limit his review of tax returns to only three years? Why? Oh, because plaintiff's counsel only gave them three years of returns and did not give the earlier returns showing much greater earnings?

Similarly, the assumptions made or not made and the reasons for the assumptions can be critical. Was she asked to assume the plaintiff could never work again? Did the expert suggest that she could and should prepare an alternative model that included earnings based on a different, less demanding job, and was the expert then told not to prepare that model? Did the expert send plaintiff's counsel a detailed survey for completion by plaintiff, only to be told that it was not needed? And wouldn't the expert agree that God only knows what his opinion might have been had he received the completed survey?

Does the expert's opinion depend on the work or opinions of other experts that the economist has not been able to verify? And, indeed, has the economist been asked to rely upon opinions of others that are totally invalid from an economic viewpoint because they rely upon data that is invalid for economic loss projections? For example, has the economist been asked to rely upon the report of a "job placement specialist" who has opined that the decedent, who had worked only as an office administrator, could have made X dollars working as a rocket scientist? Does the economist's opinion depend on the validity of the work of the job placement specialist? Since you assumed that the decedent could have been a rocket scientist, wouldn't you agree that as an economist, you could determine likely earnings loss based on valid economic theory, rather than basing the loss on a Google search on the internet that read "earnings of rocket scientists?"

16.7 Specific "Discovery" Areas

If not clear from the face of the economist's report, there are many specific items you must address for actual discovery purposes, simply so you will understand the report and be prepared to undermine it. This chapter provides a laundry list of those items, but fortunately, other chapters include in-depth analysis. The laundry list: What wage or income information was used, and what were the data sources? What discount rate was used for the present value calculation, and why was it used? How was the loss of fringe benefit calculated, using what data? What was the basis for the loss of services claim, what personal consumption rate was used, and why?

16.8 The Dilemma: Do You Use a Defense Economist?

Defense lawyers are invariably presented with two hard questions, especially in cases of questionable liability. If I use a defense economist, will the jury assume that means the defense concedes liability? Is there the risk that the defense will cure the deficiencies in the testimony of plaintiff's economist, providing the jury a basis for an accurate damage calculation?

While those questions are here posed, they are not here answered. Defense lawyers have debated for decades and will continue to debate the question of whether using a defense economist at trial will be treated by jurors as a liability concession. Many great defense lawyers answer with an emphatic "yes," while other great defense lawyers answer with an emphatic "no." There is no clearcut answer and you must form your own judgment in each case. However, one conclusion is universally true: unless you personally have training in economics, hire an economic consultant to help you prepare for plaintiff's economist. Reserve to a later day the question of whether that consultant will become a testifying expert. Similarly, whether your trial economist will fill the gap left by the plaintiff's economist is a case-by-case issue, to be decided only after you have cross-examined plaintiff's economist at trial. Did you get what you wanted and needed, so you should leave well enough alone?

16.9 Preparing the Defense Economist for Deposition

The tips for preparation of your economist for deposition are simple. Prepare yourself just like you were going to cross-examine plaintiff's economist, then prepare your expert based on the cross-examination she will face. Get your expert's writings, get her reports, get her depositions, and make sure you know what data she has used.

16.10 Trial Considerations
A. Pretrial

Beginning at the beginning, the first question that arises is whether you should file a motion to exclude or limit the testimony of plaintiff's economist based on your excellent deposition. Again, there is no one answer. If you file the motion and win before trial, will the judge grant a continuance, permitting plaintiff to get a new expert? Yes? Then don't file the motion until just before the witness takes the stand (assuming your judge won't then cut off your legs). If you file the motion, are you likely to lose, while having educated your opponent as to weaknesses? If so, don't file the motion. Are you in federal court, and are the opinions so lacking in factual foundation that you are likely to win the *Daubert* motion? Yes? File the motion.

If a punitive damages claim is asserted and your jurisdiction permits bifurcation, should you bifurcate? If your jurisdiction is one that completely bifurcates evidence of liability and damages for punitive damages from liability for actual damages, probably so. If your jurisdiction is one in which evidence is presented for liability on both actual and punitive damages, with the bifurcated phase doing nothing more that determining amount, with the only evidence presented being the financial condition of the defendant, think it through. Will that financial evidence in Phase I make it more likely there will be a finding of liability, weighing in favor of asking for bifurcation? Or, instead, will a separate damages phase simply emphasize how rich your client is, weighing against bifurcation?

B. Jury selection

How about jury selection? Do you discuss damages? Yes, at least in a general context. Does the venire understand they must first determine liability before deciding damages? Do they understand damage amounts are not to be influenced by sympathy? Are they disabled? Are they willing to use their common sense, or will they automatically believe anything an economist says about damages?

Whether case-specific questions should be asked during jury selection is again a case-by-case judgment call, usually determined by deciding whether the damage claim asserted is extreme or unreasonable. In that instance, you might want to ask, "Are there any of you who suffered a broken arm and never worked again the rest of your life? Do you think you can fairly and impartially listen to evidence from plaintiff's expert economist who has projected a total wage loss for the next forty-five years because of plaintiff's broken arm?"

C. Opening statement

Again, the dilemma, with no clear answer, is whether you do or do not discuss damages. Bear in mind, however, there are ways for a defense lawyer to discuss damages without discussing damages! "You will hear testimony from plaintiff's own economic expert that when determining the amount of lost wages for thirty years, as is the case here, the principles that govern economists require the economist to consider what the plaintiff earned in the past, going back as far as possible. But you will hear evidence that plaintiff's economist was instructed by the plaintiff's own lawyers to ignore plaintiff's twenty-year work and earnings history."

Should the defense lawyer mention the defense expert, either by saying a defense economist will be called, or mentioning the economist by name? If the case is a damages case only, probably. If the case is a liability case as well, usually not. The defense lawyer can make the necessary points without talking about the defense economist, since many of the things that the defense economist will say are likely to also be said during the cross-examination of plaintiff's economist. In opening, talk about those general propositions with which plaintiff's economist agreed during deposition, explaining how the economist then ignored those propositions. While you are talking about damages, you are also undermining the credibility of the entire case, permitting later closing argument that "you have not heard the true story. You did not hear the truth about how the accident happened. You did not hear the truth about the injuries. And you heard the incredible claim that a broken arm has resulted in $1 million in future lost wages. If one card falls, the entire house falls."

D. Lay witnesses

Lay witnesses are an often-overlooked source of impeachment of the testimony from plaintiff's economist. The economist has projected wage loss; it is now eight years post accident, and the economic report projects that plaintiff should now be making $59,000 per year. When his fellow truck driver is on the stand explaining how hard it is to drive a truck with a broken arm, consider asking, "Oh, by the way, you and Mr. Jones worked for the same company, doing the same job? How much money did you make last year as a truck driver for the company? Oh, $41,000? So, the suggestion that Mr. Jones would have made $59,000 as a truck driver this year just isn't right, is it?"

E. Cross-examining plaintiff's economist

What are the goals of cross-examining the plaintiff's economist? First, the defense lawyer wants to destroy the credibility of the calculations. Second, if possible, the defense lawyer wants to turn plaintiff's economist into a defense witness, with plaintiff's own economist recalculating the loss in defendant's favor.

How are those goals accomplished? A guaranteed formula for insuring that the goals are *not* achieved is by trying to "out-expert" the expert. The very second a lawyer asks a question chock full of technical economic jargon, doom is probable. When you ask, "Wouldn't you agree with me that the Federal Reserve has historically established rates for treasury bills based on conservative market theory dependent on variables that are not always observed in free markets," you have done two things. First, you have totally lost the jury. Second, you have invited ambush. The economist knows economic terms far better than you and when he responds to the technical question, not only does the expert sound far more knowledgeable, even if you have "won," the jury won't know it.

Ask simple, easily understood questions that sell your themes, based on the commitments you received in the deposition. "Ma'am, you would agree with me that the best way to determine the loss of household services is the completion of a detailed questionnaire that explains everything the plaintiff did around the house before the accident and how much time she spent doing it? In fact, you think that source of information is so important, that you sent a questionnaire to plaintiff's counsel, asking for that very information. But, you were not given that information before you wrote your report? You were not given that information before I took your deposition? And you weren't given that information before you got up here to today to testify? So, you have not seen that information and it sure isn't here for the jury to see?"

Defense counsel should also demonstrate the extremes and then use the plaintiff's expert to recalculate the loss based on reality. For example, defense counsel might ask, "Sir, you assumed that Mr. Jones' wages would increase 15 percent per year for the remainder of his life, correct? Now, Mr. Jones was making $32,000 at the time of the accident. Let's take a look at your projection as to what Mr. Jones might be making in fourteen years. Am I right that you project that fourteen years from now Mr. Jones would be making $169,000 a year? And that by the time of retirement age, Mr. Jones would be making $452,000 a year?

And that's all based on a pay raise of 15 percent each year? But as we discussed earlier, if you had considered the twenty-year employment history, Mr. Jones pay only increased 1.2 percent per year. And, let's run this number together—if you use 1.2 percent, you would agree with me that in fourteen years, Mr. Jones would be making $36,200? And if the 1.2 percent number is correct, you overstated future earnings by over $130,000, just for one year alone?"

How do you conclude the cross? You end where you started, demonstrating that the economist has simply made a prediction, that predictions come true only 50 percent of the time, that the prediction is based on assumptions, that if one assumption is wrong the calculations are wrong (garbage in, garbage out), and that if reality is substituted for garbage, the loss is ten times less than stated.

F. The defense economist

Should you call the defense expert as a live witness? Only if you conclude that your cross-examination of plaintiff's expert did not persuasively convince the jury that the plaintiff's economist should be totally ignored or if you conclude that it is important to put a specific damage number in front of the jury that you were not able to persuasively get before the jury during cross-examination of plaintiff's expert.

Assuming you have answered the question by deciding to call your own expert, the rules are fairly simple. Ask simple questions and get simple answers. Hold down the techno-speak. Let your expert teach. Have your expert explain the assumptions he made, demonstrating how those assumptions are actually supported by the evidence. Consider having your expert run two sets of numbers, both of which he will present to the jury. The first set of numbers includes the bottom line number he believes is appropriate, based on valid assumptions. The second set of numbers is based on certain assumptions made by plaintiff's economist which your economist does not accept, but which a jury might. For example, your economist may believe that a certain discount rate should be used, while the plaintiff's expert has testified that a different discount rate should be used. You may then inquire of your own expert, "Dr. X, you used a discount rate of Y in your calculations. You will recall that plaintiff's economist used a discount rate of Z. While I know you do not agree with that discount rate, did I ask you to also run your calculations using that discount rate? And, by using that discount rate that you think is an incorrect one, have you given plaintiff every benefit of the doubt? What was the result of that calculation?"

Prepare your expert for cross-examination by having your partner cross-examine him before trial. Identify weaknesses and retool your thinking and your questions. Address those weaknesses on direct examination, depriving plaintiff of the opportunity. Make sure your expert understands that even on cross-examination, she should continue to teach and speak simply. Explain that the expert need not get combative or defensive, and that if something is asked that needs further explanation, it will be handled on redirect examination. On a note of caution, however, remember that unless properly handled, redirect examination does nothing more than emphasize the points made by your opponent.

G. Closing argument

The dilemma presented at the beginning of the case is presented at the end. Do you argue damages? There are great lawyers who say to never argue damages in a questionable liability case, while there are other great lawyers who suggest that you must argue damages and that jurors are not confused and do not consider damages arguments as a confession of liability.

Although there are no clear answers, it must again be remembered that there are ways to argue damages without arguing damages. Skilled advocates can address damages by using the testimony of plaintiff's economist to undermine the credibility of plaintiff's case on an overall basis. Similarly, skilled advocates can use the testimony of plaintiff's economist to give the jury a "lower number" without watering down the liability defenses. "Folks, Mr. X, plaintiff's own economist, told you that he ignored the actual pay raises that were received out at the XY Trucking Company. Remember that he projected that Mr. Jones would be making $59,000 per year right now, today, when we know from Mr. Smith, the fellow who also worked at XY, that truck drivers are only making $36,000 per year. Why would you say $59,000 when it is $36,000? For the same reason you would say the light was green when every other witness says it was red. Mrs. Brown is not liable for Mr. Jones' injuries, but even if she were, plaintiff's own economist has told you that the real number for lost wages is $99,000, not $999,000."

Defense lawyers must bear in mind that the calculations from plaintiff's economist are usually based on the assumption that plaintiff either will never work again, or, if plaintiff works again, that it will be at a much lower paying job. Defense counsel should explain to the jury that the assumption is not accurate, not only because plaintiff did not tell the truth to the doctors, but also because today's society is one of great technological advancement. Remember that the computers used to send Apollo 13 to the Moon had less memory and capability than today's handheld computers. Also remember that with today's technology, science and medicine improve daily. Indeed, defense counsel can provide examples of diseases that have been cured in just the last ten years, rendering invalid the opinion of an expert given eleven years ago that a plaintiff could never again work.

Finally, in those cases in which plaintiff seeks large awards, defense counsel should be prepared to explain what it is that plaintiff really seeks to do—recover vast sums of money, far beyond the earnings potential of plaintiff, while adding plaintiff's survivors to the list of multimillionaires. "You heard that Mr. Jones never made more than $75,000 per year in his entire life. Yet, you have been asked to return a verdict for $10 million. Let's think about that. $10 million placed in certificates of deposit that earn only 5 percent interest would give plaintiff $500,000 per year—almost seven times more per year than plaintiff ever earned. And that's without even touching the money, so that Mr. Jones' wife or children would then inherit $10 million after he dies. And they would then earn $500,000 per year—and leave their children $10 million. On the other hand, if you award $3 million, Mr. Jones would earn at least $150,000 per year—twice as much money as he has ever made—and still leave $3 million to his family."

16.11 Conclusion

By now, it is likely that you, the reader, have reached the most obvious conclusion on your own—with a couple of exceptions, "defense" damage issues are not significantly different that "plaintiff's issues." Rather, the issues are issues of strategy and advocacy. The rules for preparation for deposition and trial cross-examination are basically the same, regardless of the party represented. However, defense counsel must always remember the goal—defeat or minimize damages. While the road map used by plaintiff's counsel and defense counsel may be the same, making the correct turn at the correct intersection is the real challenge.

Chapter 17

International Issues in Economic Damages

John O. Ward, Ph.D. and Robert J. Thornton, Ph.D.

17.1 Overview

Damages experts and attorneys can encounter international issues in personal injury or death litigation in three situations: (1) you are calculating damages for a foreign national, wrongfully injured or killed in the United States, (2) you are calculating damages for a U.S. national wrongfully injured or killed in a foreign country with jurisdiction in a foreign country or the U.S., or (3) you are calculating damages for a foreign national wrongfully injured or killed in a foreign country or in international airspace or waters with jurisdiction in the United States. The first situation is fairly common and is the focus of this chapter. The second situation is rare and usually involves airplane accidents involving U.S. airlines or cruise ships in international air or waters or products liability cases involving U.S. manufacturers. The third situation involves foreign nationals on U.S. carriers or product liability as described in situation two. A fourth situation, involving a foreign national with jurisdiction in a foreign country would very rarely be encountered, but the issues of such calculations are discussed briefly here and in the CD attachment to this chapter.

17.2 The Foreign National Plaintiff in the U.S.

In the case of a foreign national tourist or business person wrongfully injured or killed in the United States, the calculation of economic loss, by necessity, would be predicated on the use of statistics and data drawn from that individual's home nation. A projection of lost earnings would therefore be based on earnings in that nation, the growth rates of earnings in that nation, fringe benefits, discount rates, and costs of services in that nation. The cost of future medical care would be based on costs in that nation. The case would be tried using U.S. rules on such issues as collateral sources and the admission of testimony on the taxability of loss, usually in federal court. As an example, for a wrongful injury suffered by a visitor from Mexico, the costs of care in Mexico, the replacement wage for household services, the levels of wages and their growth would all be based on data from Mexico. The problems involved in projecting economic losses in such cases are considerable. Few countries maintain the variety of statistical databases on earnings, earnings growth, unemployment, mortality, and morbidity found in the United States. If the data necessary to make a reasonable forecast of economic loss is not available for the plaintiff's country of origin, the economist might use appropriate databases from the United States, with modifications where necessary. For example, age earnings data are typically only available for highly developed countries. It is reasonable, however, to believe that the same earnings trends would exist in other nations than the U.S. Average hours of household services performed using U.S. surveys might relate to other industrial nations, but be inappropriate for use in a country like Mexico, where wages of service workers are very low and such services are less frequently performed by middle and high income families. The same issues arise in the treatment of the wrongful death or injury of any foreign resident in the United States.

A distinction must be made between legal and illegal resident status. The calculation of damages for a legal resident might be much the same as that for a U.S. citizen, especially when the legal resident worker has lived in the U.S. for a number of years. Nevertheless, questions about which national life tables to use, the cost of future medical care when the individual may return to their country of origin, and other actuarial concerns must be addressed. The length of time spent in the United States will determine the degree to which you can use U.S. actuarial and wage data in the calculation or such data from the plaintiff's home country. The U.S. has a rich base of actuarial data for population and workers to draw upon for probabilities of death, unemployment, disability, wage growth and levels of household services. Such data are also easily accessed for Canada and the European Union countries, and are comparable to such data in the United States.

Finding such actuarial data for Mexico and nations in Central America, South America, Africa and Asia is much more problematic. Such data are often not collected systematically, and the detail of the data is usually limited to gross measures such as all males or females. In the appendix to this chapter we provide website information on data sources for Canada and Mexico, the two largest sources of immigrants to the U.S. More general sources of international labor and actuarial data would include:

- *International Financial Statistics,* International Monetary Fund
  http://www.imf.org/external/pubind.htm
- *World Tables,* World Bank http://www.worldbank.org/data
- *Statistical Yearbook,* United Nations
  http://unstats.un.org/unsd/pubs/gesgrid.asp?id=368
- *Yearbook of Labour Statistics,* International Labour Organization
  http://www.ilo.org
- *The Statistical Guide to Europe,* European Commission
  http://ec.europa.eu/index_en.htm

Because of the difficulty of finding reliable and detailed data for population and workers in Mexico and Central America, the largest sources of foreign national workers in the United States, the reliability of forensic economic forecast models using such data is diminished, as are the outcomes of vocational rehabilitation appraisals and life care plans. For the plaintiff, the resulting loss forecasts are inevitability much lower than such forecasts using U.S. data. For the legal resident worker, the defense will stress the need to treat the individual as a foreign worker, using the national data appropriate to the worker's origin as a base for calculating loss. Our experience has been that such efforts usually fail and the calculations are based on U.S. data. Such is not the case with illegal workers.

For the illegal national employed in the United States, issues of damages are even more uncertain. Some states, such as Texas, have specified that losses must be based on the assumption the individual would have returned to their country of origin. As such, wage loss, value of services, and future medical costs would be calculated using wages and costs represented by the country of origin. Similarly, actuarial data on unemployment, disability, and death probabilities would have to come from the country of origin. In a Kansas case, *Hernandez-Cortez v. Hernandez,* 2003 U.S. Dist.Lexis 19780 (D. Kansas 2003), a judge granted summary judgment to the defendant on the issue that lost earnings for the illegal aliens could not be based on wage and life expectancy data in the U.S. as the economist preparing damages for the plaintiffs had done. In other states this bar to damages is less clear, and where the individual has worked in the United States for many years, the analysis becomes more complex, especially with the prospect of "forgiveness" periodically given to illegal aliens. The most recent general amnesty was given to aliens who could verify that they resided in the U.S. since 1982. In the appendix to this chapter we have attached a brief submitted by the Washington Legal Foundation in the California case of *Paramount v. Superior Court* decided in 2006 and a web page discussing the current treatment of illegal workers in Texas and Florida.

The largest single group of foreign nationals working in the United States comes from Mexico. In 2003, the Immigration and Naturalization Service estimated that 33.5 million foreign-born persons lived in the United States and that 9 million were illegal immigrants who had entered illegally or overextended their stay. The Department of Homeland Security puts the number of illegal immigrants at more than 11 million in 2006. More than half are estimated to have come from Mexico. A detailed breakdown of the growth of immigration, legal and illegal, is contained on the CD for this chapter. In addition to foreign residents (legal and illegal), millions of visitors come to the United States each year as tourists or for business.

17.3 The Foreign National in the Foreign Country with U.S. Jurisdiction

In the *Bridgestone Tire* litigation, for example, a number of residents of Mexico, Venezuela and other Latin American countries were injured or died and lawsuits were filed against U.S. manufacturers in U.S. federal courts. The calculation of damages in such cases would proceed using specific wage and actuarial data drawn from the foreign country. It is very difficult to get such products liability cases to U.S. federal courts, but the potential damages from such cases are substantial. Other such cases might include cruise ship passengers or air crash or cruise ship victims on U.S. carriers.

17.4 The U.S. National or Foreign National in a Foreign Country with Foreign Jurisdiction

While the damages expert might be involved in such cases, the U.S. Attorney typically would not be directly involved because of jurisdiction and differing litigation procedures. Damages center on what will be allowed as damages and how they can be calculated. Damages calculations in Canada are much the same as in the United States with some notable exceptions in Quebec Province. In addition, such actions typically occur before judges rather than juries. The same is true in the E.U., where damages are usually established by statute and damages schedules, much like workers' compensation. An overview of the use of scheduled damages tables in the U.K. and Ireland, along with the court systems of the U.K., Ireland, and Canada, are contained in the CD.

17.5 Summary

The use of damages experts in wrongful personal injury and death actions will require a clarification of what rules of law apply and what assumptions about nation of residence are permissible. When the experts must assume that the plaintiff's home country must form the basis of assumptions about life expectancy, wages, value of services, life care costs and all actuarial adjustments to the projections, the analysis becomes more complex and less certain. It is essential to clarify the assumed nation of residence for the purposes of the calculation. For the defense, it is essential to contest a plaintiff's assumption that they would have remained in the United States, subject to U.S. actuarial assumptions. For the plaintiff, arguments that the individual would have remained in the United States, gained citizenship or immunity should be advanced. In any event, the damages expert should know the data sources for national actuarial data and the rules of evidence to be used.

About the Editors

Michael L. Brookshire, Ph.D. is a Professor of Economics at the Marshall University Graduate College in Charleston, West Virginia, and the President of Michael L. Brookshire and Associates. His doctorate in economics is from the University of Tennessee, Knoxville, and much of his early career was spent as an executive officer of the University of Tennessee and the University of Cincinnati. Dr. Brookshire has authored two books and over thirty-five refereed articles and book chapters on the proper calculation of economic damages. He has worked for plaintiff and defense attorneys in such notable cases as the Arrow Air (Gander, Newfoundland) and Lockerbie (Scotland) airplane crash cases and such class action cases as the Fen-Phen, Bendectin, E. I. du Pont C-8, and Tobacco Smoker cases. Dr. Brookshire was a charter member of the National Association of Forensic Economics (NAFE) and served on the Board of Directors from 1990-2001. He served as the fifth president of the Association in 1993–1994 and as the second, executive director of the Association from 1999–2001. He received in 1999 the past presidents' award for outstanding service to the Association.

Frank Slesnick, Ph.D. received his B.A. from Oberlin College and Ph.D. in Economics from the University of Minnesota. He taught at Denison University in Granville, Ohio, and for thirty years at Bellarmine University in Louisville, Kentucky. In addition to his full-time duties as a professor of economics, he has served as a forensic economic consultant for twenty-five years in the area of personal injury/death cases with a specific focus on medical cost issues. Dr. Slesnick has published widely in the field of forensic economics and currently serves as an Associate Editor of the *Journal of Forensic Economics*. In 1991–92, he served as the fourth President of the National Association of Forensic Economics. He retired from teaching in 2005 but maintains an active consulting practice.

John O. Ward, Ph.D. is Professor Emeritus of Economics at the University of Missouri-Kansas City (UMKC) and President of John Ward Economics, a litigation consulting firm located in Prairie Village, Kansas. Dr. Ward has a B.A. and M.A. in Economics from the University of Toledo and a Ph.D. from the University of Oklahoma, granted in 1970. Dr. Ward was a professor of economics at

UMKC from 1969 to 2003, serving as Department Chair for fourteen years and Associate Dean of the College of Arts and Sciences for eight years. He continues to teach Human Resource Economics and Law and Economics for graduate students. His publications include five edited or authored books, fifty-three papers published in refereed journals, publications in law journals and reviews and numerous presentations at national and international academic and professional meetings. Dr. Ward was the first President of the National Association of Forensic Economics and the founding editor of the *Journal of Forensic Economics*. He served as editor of that journal until 2004, when he became editor emeritus. Dr. Ward has served as a consultant for the Department of Labor, the Department of Defense, the governments of Brazil and Mexico and numerous non-profit organizations, including the American Epilepsy Association and the Families of September 11th Association. Dr. Ward's consulting firm, John Ward Economics, employs eight economists and staff. The firm provides economic litigation support in commercial litigation, employment law, anti-trust and personal injury and death litigation throughout the United States.

About the Authors

George A. Barrett, M.B.A., M.S.R.C., C.R.C., C.V.E. received his B.A. in Economics from West Virginia State University, his M.B.A. from Marshall University, and his M.S. in Rehabilitation Counseling from West Virginia University. Mr. Barrett is the 1995 recipient of the Gold Key Outstanding Student Leadership Award from *Omicron Delta Epsilon*, the International Honor Society in Economics. Mr. Barrett began his professional career as a product cost projection analyst with a national food wholesaler and following this was the coordinator of student assessment at West Virginia State University where he remained until entering private forensic practice with Michael L. Brookshire & Associates in Charleston, West Virginia. He has served as an adjunct instructor of macroeconomics at West Virginia State University. In addition, he has presented research findings at numerous national economic conferences and published articles in several peer-reviewed journals. Currently, Mr. Barrett is a referee of the *Journal of Forensic Economics* and also serves an administrative function for the National Association of Forensic Economics as co-owner of the organization's e-mail list serve. In addition to economic expertise, Mr. Barrett is a vocational rehabilitation consultant and holds certifications as a Certified Rehabilitation Counselor and Certified Vocational Evaluation Specialist.

Elizabeth A.W. Gunderson, Ph.D. is Professor and Chair of the Management and Economics Department at Hamline University in St. Paul, Minnesota, where she has taught for over twenty-six years. In addition to her full-time duties as a professor, Dr. Gunderson has served as a forensic economic consultant for over sixteen years, primarily in the areas of personal injury, wrongful death and employment discrimination. She has published in the field of forensic economics and has served as a Vice President At-Large of the National Association of Forensic Economics.

John D. Hancock, Ph.D. is a consulting economist with his own firm, Economic & Financial Analysis, in Sacramento, California. He specializes in forensic economics, business valuation, antitrust, contracts, and patent infringement. He has been the project manager of several State of California research projects.

Dr. Hancock is a full-time member of the Adjunct Faculty at the University of California at Davis. Dr. Hancock regularly participates as a reviewer for several academic journals. He holds a Doctorate degree in Economics from Purdue University, a Master's of Economics from Purdue University, and a Bachelor's Degree in Economics from Indiana University.

R. Edison Hill, Esq. received his law degree from West Virginia University College of Law in 1976. He founded the law firm of Hill, Peterson, Carper, Bee & Deitzler, P.L.L.C. in June 1980, after leaving a large corporate law firm where he had worked as an associate for three years. Mr. Hill is a trial lawyer and exclusively represents plaintiffs in civil matters. He has been involved in representing clients suffering from various types of injuries, including those from toxic chemical exposure. He and his law firm are involved on behalf of plaintiffs in mass tort actions and class actions. In 2005, he was awarded the Trial Lawyer of the Year Award by Trial Lawyers for Public Justice for successful class action litigation in the case of *Leach, et al. v. E. I. du Pont de Nemours and Company,* which case involved drinking water contamination by a chemical utilized in the manufacture of Teflon. Mr. Hill is a Life Member of American Association for Justice, and he is a former president of the West Virginia Trial Lawyers Association. He is Board certified as a Civil Trial Advocate by the National Board of Trial Advocacy.

Kurt V. Krueger, Ph.D. is an economist at John Ward Economics in Prairie Village, Kansas. He specializes in forensic economics and economic demography. He serves as an associate editor for the *Journal of Forensic Economics* in the area of empirical reviews. He was the Southern Vice President for the National Association of Forensic Economics from 2004 to 2006. Dr. Krueger has been an adjunct professor and lecturer at two Kansas City area universities and he was a past research assistant at the Institute for Public Policy and Business Research at the University of Kansas. He has published in the *Journal of Forensic Economics, Litigation Economics Digest, Litigation Economics Review,* and *The Earnings Analyst.* He has also published several economic research reports, has numerous book chapters, and a book on catastrophic injury damages. Dr. Krueger regularly participates in academic program sessions sponsored by the National Association of Forensic Economics and the American Academy of Economic and Financial Experts. He holds a Doctorate degree in Economics from the University of Missouri-Kansas City, a Master's of Economics from the University of Kansas, and a Bachelor's of Science in Economics from the University of Kansas.

Gerald Martin, M.B.A., Ph.D. received his B.S. from Clemson University and his M.B.A. and Ph.D. from Arizona State University. His Ph.D. was earned in the field of Finance. He has taught as a tenured professor at several universities and began his forensic economic consulting practice in 1973. He has been retained in over 4,000 cases in sixteen states and has testified in approximately 1,400 of those cases. Dr. Martin has over 100 publications and presentations and is the author of *Determining Economic Damages* (James Publishing, Inc.), a guidebook on forensic economics that has been updated annually since 1988. He has served on the Board of Directors of the National Association of Forensic Economics and the American Rehabilitation Economics Association. His consulting specialties are personal injury, wrongful death, and wrongful termination and he is one of a limited number of economists certified by the Department of Health and Human Services to evaluate Vaccine Act cases.

Ann T. Neulicht, Ph.D., C.L.C.P., C.R.C., C.V.E., C.D.M.S., L.P.C., D-ABVE earned her Doctorate in Rehabilitation Research and has over twenty years of experience as a Rehabilitation Counselor, case manager, vocational expert, life care planner, and educator. She is the Vocational Counselor for the Work-Life Readiness Program for Start-Up Adults at the UNC-CH Center for Development and Learning, serves as a Vocational Expert for the Social Security Administration and has qualified as a Rehabilitation and/or Life Care Planning Expert in Workers' Compensation Hearings as well as superior, district, and federal court. She is a 2005 IARP (International Association or Rehabilitation Professionals) appointee to the Commission on Rehabilitation Counselor Certification, and is a past NARPPS Forensic Section Co-Chair, Chair, and Region IV Representative to the Board of Directors. She has been honored with the IARP Outstanding Individual Professional Member Award, as well as the Distinguished Service and Harley B. Reger Awards from the National Rehabilitation Counseling Association. Dr. Neulicht is a principal investigator in the Life Care Plan Survey 2001 and Labor Market Research Survey (2006). Her interest in ethics, rehabilitation/life care plan practices, and forensic issues has led to several publications and multiple presentations at local, regional, and national conferences.

Jeffrey B. Opp received his B.A. in Economics from the University of Denver, and served as an Infantry Officer in the United States Army Reserve. As managing partner of Caulson, Opp & Associates, P.C., he has specialized in financial litigation support for over eighteen years, and has testified hundreds of times in courts throughout the United States. Mr. Opp has determined losses resulting from the failure of several Savings and Loan Associations, and Commercial

Banking Institutions on behalf of the RTC and the FDIC. He has prepared short pay and breach of contract damages in numerous national class actions involving tens of thousands of class members. He has assisted attorneys and insurance agents in the preparation or review of thousands of lost profit claims and personal injury damage analyses including over 1,000 F.E.L.A. matters. Mr. Opp has analyzed and calculated damages in hundreds of commercial breach of contract and tort matters involving billions of dollars in assessed or claimed damages. He was a testifying expert for Federal Agencies such as the Department of Justice, Federal Bureau of Investigation, and United States Attorney.

William A. Posey, Esq. received his B.A. and J.D. from the University of Cincinnati. He is a partner with the Cincinnati, Ohio, law firm of Keating Muething & Klekamp, PLL and is the chair of its tort litigation group. Mr. Posey's practice involves all aspects of litigation with particular interest in representing plaintiffs and defendants in personal injury, product liability, medical malpractice, and aviation-related claims. He has litigated tort claims in over thirty-five states. He regularly lectures on topics relating to accident reconstruction, use of experts, and trial strategy and damages. Mr. Posey is a member of the Aircraft Owners and Pilots Bar Association, American Bar Association, Cincinnati Bar Association, Defense Research Institute, Lawyer-Pilot Bar Association, Ohio Academy of Trial Lawyers, Ohio State Bar Association, and The Association of Trial Lawyers of America.

James D. Rodgers, Ph.D. is Professor Emeritus of Economics at Penn State University. He received his Ph.D. in economics from the University of Virginia in 1970. Dr. Rodgers taught for thirty years at Penn State. He taught a variety of graduate and undergraduate courses in economics, including upper division undergraduate courses in forensic economics and the economics of accident law. His research in the area of forensic economics includes published work on economic damages in personal injury and wrongful death cases, age-earnings profiles, the personal maintenance deduction, the valuation of time spent in non-market activities, and the valuation of Social Security benefits, the valuation of pension benefits, and taxes in employment law cases; he is also the co-author of a book on expert economic testimony. Dr. Rodgers maintains an active consulting practice and has worked as an economic consultant since 1976, preparing economic damage appraisal reports and trial testimony pertaining thereto. He currently serves as an associate editor of the *Journal of Forensic Economics*. He is a past President of the National Association of Forensic Economics and a recipient of the past presidents' award for outstanding service to the Association.

E. Wayne Taff, Esq., senior shareholder of Sherman Taff Bangert Thomas & Coronado, P.C. of Kansas City, Missouri, has tried major exposure jury trials throughout the United States for thirty years, serving as national, regional, and local trial counsel for numerous corporations. In addition to his many years as a defense trial lawyer, Mr. Taff spent a number of years as a plaintiff's lawyer with millions of dollars in verdicts. He practices primarily in the areas of products liability, toxic torts, trucking law and insurance bad faith and coverage. He has lectured and published nationally and internationally on products liability, toxic torts, and trial tactics. Mr. Taff has served as Officer, Board Member, Chair of the Products Liability Committee, and Chair of the Law Institute of the Defense Research Institute, the world's largest organization of civil defense trial lawyers.

Robert H. Taylor M.A., L.P.C., C.R.C., C.D.M.S.,C.L.C.P. is president and director of Vocational Diagnostics, Inc. in Phoenix, Arizona. Mr. Taylor earned a Master's degree in Rehabilitation Counseling from New York University in 1975. He is a licensed professional counselor by the Arizona Board of Behavioral Health Examiners. He holds certifications as a rehabilitation counselor, disability management specialist and life care planner. Mr. Taylor's practice is national in scope, primarily catastrophic injury cases involving evaluation of lost wages and loss of earning capacity and life care planning for children and adults who have had traumatic brain injuries, spinal cord injuries and other catastrophic injuries. He has testified in well over 100 jury trials in both state and federal courts across the United States as an expert in vocational rehabilitation and life care planning.

Robert J. Thornton, Ph.D. is McFarlane Professor of Economics at Lehigh University in Bethlehem, Pennsylvania. He received his Ph.D. at the University of Illinois in 1970 and worked as a research assistant at the Brookings Institution. He has written and edited fifteen books and nearly 100 articles and book chapters in the fields of labor economics and forensic economics. A practicing forensic economist for about twenty-five years, he specializes in the areas of personal injury/death and discrimination. He is an associate editor of the *Journal of Forensic Economics,* and also serves as a series editor for Elsevier Press. Dr. Thornton is a past president of the National Association of Forensic Economics (1989–90).

Howard H. Vogel, Esq. is a member of the Knoxville, Tennessee, law firm of O'Neil, Parker & Williamson. He was born and grew up in Paris, Tennessee. He is a graduate of Vanderbilt University, B.A., 1971, and the University of Tennessee College of Law, J.D., 1974. He is admitted to practice in Tennessee. He has served as president of the Knoxville Bar Association and the Tennessee Bar Association. He is a former member of the ABA Board of Governors. He has chaired various ABA standing committees and is currently the State Delegate for Tennessee to the ABA House of Delegates. Mr. Vogel has been an active civil litigator but for many years has practiced as a mediator. He has mediated over 1,100 disputes and is a fellow of the International Academy of Mediators.

Index

A

accountant, 10, 17, 22, 24, 29, 107, 118
accrual, 38
Activities of Daily Living (ADLs), 76, 81
admissibility, 12-14, 19
age-earnings, 28, 104-105, 112-113
allocation, 48
allowances, 39
annuitant, 143-144
annuitist, 146-147
appellate courts, 19, 119
apportionment, 126
assets, 118

B

base earnings, 23, 25, 27-28
bifurcation, 168
Bridgestone Tire litigation, 178

C

California, 54, 90, 94-95, 132, 177
Canada, 176, 179
capital, 123-124
caregiver, 82
Carey v. Piphus, 51
catastrophic injuries, 57, 74, 82, 146
ceilings, 115
Certified Public Accountant (CPA), 23, 118
Certified Rehabilitation Counselor (CRC), 10, 55, 62, 69
Certified Vocational Evaluator (CVA), 10
Certified Vocational Expert (CVE), 10
child care, 36, 49
Collier v. Sims, 46
Consolidated Omnibus Reconciliation Act (COBRA), 36, 43

H

healthcare provider, 150-151
hedonic damages, 93, 95, 97-98, 149, 153, 160-161
Hernandez-Cortez v. Hernandez, 177
household services, see also Chapter 5, 4-5, 16, 20-21, 23, 26, 33, 81, 91, 93, 97,
    149, 151-153, 160, 170, 176
hypotheticals, 5-6, 9, 11-12, 24

I

International Academy of Life Care Planners (IALCP), 74-75
inflation, 5, 7, 15, 17, 21, 28-29, 31-32, 101-102, 104-105, 147, 150
intangible losses, 161
IRA, 103
IRS, 20, 144

J

juries, 1, 4, 6, 13, 16-18, 21, 49, 67-68, 93-94, 99, 104, 119-120, 123-124, 128,
    133, 146, 151, 153, 156-163, 166-172, 179
jurors, 17, 96-97, 99, 129, 156-162, 167, 172

K

Kansas, 177
KELYNCO, 75
Kentucky, 24, 86
Kumho Tire Co. v. Carmichael, 14, 18, 55

L

layoffs, 107, 118
life annuity, 82
life care plan, 10-11, 57, 61, 65, 70, 73-74, 76-83, 105, 141, 147-148, 158, 160
life care planner, 3, 5-6, 10-11, 53, 61, 69-70, 73-81, 83, 147, 150, 158
life expectancy, 11, 16, 20, 24, 30, 50, 73, 82, 97-98, 143-147, 152, 156, 158,
    177, 179
long-term disability (LTD), 55

M

Massachusetts, 132
Medical Care Price Index (MCPI), 80, 83
Medicare, 37, 39-40, 114
minimum wage, 65, 152
Mississippi, 94

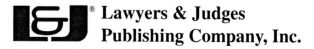
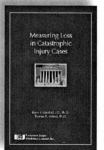

#0870 The New Hedonics Primer for Economists and Attorneys, Second Edition

Edited by Thomas R. Ireland and John O. Ward

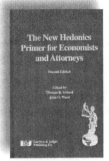

This book provides accurate and up-to-date information about the "hedonic damage" concept.

The hedonic damage concept has been used to introduce testimony from economic experts on loss of the enjoyment of life in both wrongful death and personal injury litigation. It has also recently been used to introduce testimony about "loss of society" to survivors of decedents. All of these developments are presented in a balanced format that includes papers defining, supporting, opposing and proposing alternatives to the "hedonic damage" concept in all of its applications. It also considers the impact of the 1993 *Daubert v. Merrell Dow* mandates of the U.S. Supreme Court on the future of this type of economic expert testimony.

In the past four years, a number of states have spoken on whether "hedonic damage" testimony will be permitted. A number of major cases are presented or discussed in this book. Unlike the original *Hedonics Primer for Economists and Attorneys,* this book is focused on controversies that exist within each possible use of the testimony. Several major articles have been retained from the original Primer, but most of the materials contained in the New Primer are included for the first time. In addition to updated case analysis, the book contains sample case development and other tools of importance to practitioners.

The book has been compiled and edited by John O. Ward and Thomas R. Ireland, managing editor and one of the associate editors of the *Journal of Forensic Economics,* respectively. The two fall on opposite sides of the "hedonic damages" controversy and both clearly present their own approaches and views.

Topics include:
- What are hedonic damages?
- Hedonic damages in death analysis
- Hedonic damages in personal injury analysis
- Hedonic damage and loss of society analysis
- Hedonic damages and case law
- Development of trial documents

Product Code: 0870 • Size: 6" × 9" • Casebound

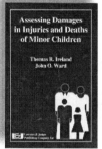

CPSIA information can be obtained
at www.ICGtesting.com
Printed in the USA
FSOW02n0547130416
19092FS